Sexual
Intimacy

Sexual
Intimacy

Andrew M. Greeley

A Crossroad Book
The Seabury Press • New York

The Seabury Press
815 Second Avenue
New York, N.Y.

Library of Congress Cataloging in Publication Data

Greeley, Andrew M   1928-
  Sexual intimacy.

  "A Crossroad book."
  1. Sexual ethics. 2. Sex (Psychology) I. Title.
HQ31.G78   1975   301.41'7   75-15558
ISBN 0-8164-2591-4

Printed in the United States of America

Contents

Sexual
Intimacy

Introduction

This book in no sense competes with Dr. David Reuben's catechism or *The Sex Book* or *The Sensuous* . . . trilogy or the research reports of Masters and Johnson. Nor is it a how-to-do-it sex manual, heaven forbid. All such books may have their appropriate function, but they all suffer from the fault that is common in behavioristic writings: they operate with a disastrously incomplete model of man.

My problem with explicit behaviorists like Masters and Johnson and implicit behaviorists like the team that put together the words and pictures of *The Sex Book* is not primarily theological or philosophical (although I have some difficulties with them in these areas too). My fundamental difference with them comes from my own social science perspective. I am in a remote sort of way a disciple of Max Weber. Hence I am convinced that what distinguishes the human from other animals is his capacity for language. The human develops symbols which enable him to give meaning and interpretation to his behavior. These meanings and interpretations are elaborated into complex cultural systems, and the patterns of behavior which are guided by such meaning systems constitute man's social structure. His interactions with others are relational in the sense that they take

9

place more or less in accordance with the norms and models provided by his culture and social structure and in the sense that he seeks personal meaning in and through his relationships. Human behavior, then, is guided by meaning systems, and human experience is interpreted by these systems. Men and women mate according to the cultural conventions of their society (though not always in precise accordance with such conventions) and they interpret their mating experience by the symbols which their culture provides for them. No other animal acts this way. The scientific observers of human sexual behavior and the wise men who offer advice on this subject (and there are always many such wise men in the marketplace) must take into account man's nature as a culture-producing and a culture-produced creature or they can't know what they are talking about.

Since humans have little in the way of instincts to prescribe what behavior is appropriate, they must fall back on the norms and conventions of the society and culture of which they are a part. These conventions may be more or less functional, more or less appropriate. If they are not subject to review and change as the circumstances in which humans find themselves change, conventions can become rigid and counterproductive. But even if old conventions are swept away (and they rarely are—the more frequent phenomenon is their gradual transformation), the result is not humans without conventions but humans with new conventions.

The behaviorists are surely right when they argue that many of the past cultural conventions on the subject of sex are not pertinent to the post-Freudian, post-Pill society. They are also correct when they suggest that some of the conventions dictated by the traditional wisdom are based on ignorance and supersition. But they are wrong if they think either that conventions can be eliminated from the human condition or that old conventions are easily abandoned. Behaviorism may have to prescind from conventions to do its laboratory research (and the ethics of this prescinding are beyond the scope of the present volume), but men and women cannot prescind from conventions (or "values," to use another word) in their sexual relationships. Books which purport to treat sexuality in a "value-free" context may be amusing, entertaining, titillating; but they will not be of much help to a creature who, whether he wants to or not, cannot help but attach values to his behavior. An authentically value-free book on sexuality (if such be possible) would be of considerable help to a chimpanzee but no help at all to a human.

So there are implicit values in the behaviorist books, and the basic one is that a person can do with his own body whatever he wants to so long as he doesn't hurt anyone else. Such a value may not be a very sophisticated ethical proposition; it is certainly neither terribly new nor very edifying, but it is at least a value. How useful it is depends on how it helps humans to make sense out of the ambiguity and confusions of their sexual behavior. Whether individualistic hedonism is much use as a value may be doubted, I think. The problem with such an implicit value as contained in the currently popular sex books is not that it is wrong, but that the books are not much help. They shed rather little light on complexities and confusions of human behavior. It is, after all, of only small moment to know how fellatio is performed and to be told that there is "nothing wrong" with it when one is always fighting with the wife and finding it difficult to keep hands off the women in the office and feeling plenty guilty about both. Nor do the details of female orgasm help much when one is trying to work up enough nerve to attempt a reconciliation in a love grown sour. It is not that orgasm is uninteresting or unimportant; it is rather that just now it is not especially pertinent.

There is no escaping the fact that the behaviorist approach to sex currently dominates the field. If one arrives at wisdom by counting noses—or the other parts of the anatomy pictured in the behaviorist books—then the value-oriented approach has obviously lost the day. But if one believes that, as John Cobb has put it, "What happens really matters only if it matters ultimately, and it matters ultimately only if it matters everlastingly," then one must dismiss the present behaviorist majority as an unfortunate and shallow historical aberration that is more a reflection on the backwardness of our time than it is on the importance of values in human behavior.

One of the reasons that the allegedly "value-free" approach to sex is so popular is that those who claim to have a "value-oriented" approach have almost universally confused interpretation with morality. In the minds of most people, to have values about sex means to be saddled with a heavy baggage of moral prohibitions. Religion's contribution to sexual behavior is to draw up a list of what ought not to be done; or, more recently, if one is to believe the approach of certain moralists, religion now provides a list of things which in fact it is all right to do despite our feelings of guilt. It remains hard for religionists, either conservative or radical, to understand that religion is not a moral code and that religious interpretation of human behavior has rather little to do with specific prohibitions or permissions. Small wonder that the behaviorists have carried the day, for even if their interpretations are both implicit and shallow, they at least go beyond casuistry.

It is the intent of this book to deal with human sexuality both in the context of the human propensity to seek meaning in behavior and from the viewpoint of a particular religious meaning system—that of a schismatic Jewish sect founded by an obscure Galilean preacher named Jesus. It will not be a morality book; I shall make no judgment on the many current issues of sexual morality which trouble the followers of Jesus, and particularly that branch which in some fashion or other and with greater or lesser enthusiasm professes loyalty to the Bishop of Rome. As I have indicated in another book, I don't think Christianity is especially interested in the morality business; it has other and better things to do, such as providing answers to the most basic questions of meaning that a man can ask. I shall not address myself to questions of birth control or premarital sex but to the question of what light the Christian symbols throw on the ambiguity and confusion that humans experience in their sex lives. The book, then, is not a manual, not a clinical portrait, and surely not a series of answers to questions you always wanted to ask. It is rather an exercise in interpretation based on the assumption that however important clinical information may be—and it is important—it is not nearly so important as interpretation.

By way of ending this introduction I wish to note that I have been a convinced feminist for a decade and a half—long before it became fashionable. I fully endorse all the goals of the feminist movement (though not all the rhetoric of some of its more bizarre advocates). But I will not waste time in this book dialoguing with those women who pick up every volume written by a male with the conviction that he is a sexist and then proceed to twist his words to prove their conviction. Obviously I cannot write about the sexuality of women as well as a woman could because I am not a woman. Nor am I well informed about the nature of female sexual fantasy because, again, I am not a woman and because there is little written material on this subject —which is most unfortunate. Yet because I am not a woman will not prevent me from saying something about the subject of human sexuality, which however much it may differ in the male and the female of the species still is human and not uniquely masculine or feminine.

Nor will I waste my time commenting on those who will say that celibates know nothing about sexuality.

1

Friendship and Marriage

I have the impression that theologizing about sexuality and marriage has ground to a halt in the Roman Church. The trauma of the encyclical letter *Humanae Vitae* has been profoundly discouraging, and what little theologizing occurs is usually either explicitly or implicitly a dialogue with *Humanae Vitae* or a reaction against the old, rigid, and inflexible approach to sexuality of which *Humanae Vitae* may well have been the last dying gasp. It is the easiest thing in the world to ridicule the theories about the role of the man and the role of the woman, which were once so much the staple of pre-Cana conferences. It is also relatively easy to repeat the argument of the contextualists in favor of premarital or extramarital sex or homosexuality (and ignore the fact that most adults are heterosexuals who do not plan extramarital relationships). But arguing with *Humanae Vitae* or ridiculing the old or justifying what previously would have been thought of as aberrant is scarcely a constructive theology. I propose to indicate a direction in which some of our theologizing might go. I am not saying that I have developed a complete theory of sexuality and marriage, nor that this is the only direction in which theorizing about marriage might go. I merely suggest that an analysis of the dynamics of human friendship and an inspection of the Christian symbols which illumine the friendship relationship might be one profitable way of approaching sexuality and marriage.

Let me begin by explicating a number of my basic assumptions:

1. Sexuality in man is human; that is to say, while it is rooted in the physical and the genital, it permeates the whole personality.

2. All human relationships are sexual; the more intimate they are, the more sexual they become.

3. There is no reason why human intimacy must terminate in genitality, though obviously there is always a radical possibility of this happening.

4. Sexuality is exchange; it is a rhythm of giving and receiving, of taking and being taken, though this rhythm is, of course, not subject to strict economic barter.

5. Marriage is a special kind of sexual intimacy. It is a permanent (or quasi-permanent) genital relationship between a man and a woman. It is the most difficult but also the most rewarding form of intimacy. It is the most difficult because of the physical and psychological complexities involved in such a close relationship between two human beings; it is the most rewarding because there is great physical and psychological pleasure in working out these difficulties.

6. Marriage is both the source and the model of all human friendships. It is the source because the capacity to take and to be taken in the marriage relationship is the most primal of man's social behaviors. It is the model because the love between husband and wife is at least the implicit ideal for all other human friendships. The problems which plague all human relationships are to be found in a special way in marriage; but the joys of all human

intimacy are also found in marriage in a special way.

7. I therefore define friendship as intimate relationship between two human beings in which both become sufficiently open to one another that they are able, at least to some extent, to put aside their fears and suspicions and enjoy the pains and the pleasures of vulnerability. Living with friendship and living with sexuality is essentially the art of living with our capacity for intimacy, with both the demands intimacy makes and the rewards it gives.

8. While friendship is presently the ideal for the marriage relationship, it has not always been so. In the past, many and perhaps most marriages were able to survive in the absence of friendship as I have defined it. Even in the present time many marriages are not in fact friendship relationships. I am not suggesting that in the pre-Freudian era there were few couples who became friends; I say only that society did not hold this up as a critical ideal. The paradox of our own time is that now friendship has become the unquestioned ideal for the marriage relationship, but the human race has not, I think, developed sufficient abilities at friendship to guarantee that married couples may achieve that ideal.

9. The relationship between friendship and marriage moves in both directions: not all marriages are friendships and not all friendships are marriages. But friendship is the ideal for marriage, and a married friendship is the model for all human relationships. I speak of friendship and marriage interchangeably, leaving aside the fascinating but highly complex question of the sexual component of human intimacies (across sexual lines or within the same sex) that are not oriented toward genital relationships. (Herbert Richardson's most recent book has some fascinating observations to make on this subject.) We may take it that since man is a composite of body and spirit, there is no psychic intimacy without some sort of physical intimacy

and that there is no physical intimacy, at least not for a long period of time, without a strain toward psychic intimacy.

10. Finally, I assume that the ideal human personality is androgynous, that is to say, it is a personality which has been able to develop both the so-called "masculine" and the so-called "feminine" potentialities within it. Given our culture, this means, I take it, that a man can be secure enough in his masculinity to permit the feminine aspects of his personality to emerge, and a woman be secure enough in her femininity to permit the masculine aspects of her personality to emerge. For most people, one must assume, this can only happen in marriage. (Which is not, be it noted, the same thing as saying that in most marriages it does happen.)

With this somewhat lengthy preliminary, let me turn to a number of assertions about friendship: 1. *Friendship is risk-taking.* Even the mildest form of human intimacy involves risk, because in intimacy we both take and are taken, we both expose ourselves to the other and reach out to possess the other. If one looks through the long series of activities which constitute the developmental process of a human marriage, we note that it is marked by a number of ventures into that which was previously unknown: dating, courtship, engagement, the marriage event, the development of bodily openness necessary in the genital component of the relationship, the much more difficult development of interpersonal openness for the psychic component of the relationship. Each of these turning points in a developing relationship involves risks, sometimes small ones, sometimes serious risks; and of course the whole process itself is an ongoing risk. Once it ceases to be so, once it has become a relationship that is both complacent and routine, it has lost its capacity for growth and its capacity to maintain the interest and involvement of the partners. Once a marriage, or indeed any friendship, ceases to be a mutual exploration of the complexities of self and other it becomes a bore.

But there is risk in such mutual exploration, for there is risk in taking and being taken. Suppose that one yields to the other and permits him to take one. What, then, if everything is taken? What if there is nothing left? What if one is unable to respond because everything has been given? There is great vulnerability in permitting oneself to be taken. Courage is required throughout the development of any human relationship, and great amounts of it are required at the critical turning points.

And there is equal and perhaps greater vulnerability in taking. What if one reaches out for the other and the other will not respond? What if one attempts to take and the other refuses to be taken? What if one exposes one's need for the other only to be rejected? There is perhaps more risk in taking than in being taken because the taking partner plays the more active role and looks more foolish and ridiculous when he is rejected. Indeed, the fear of appearing ridiculous is one of the more powerful obstacles to human intimacy. I suspect that the reason why so little of the potential of most human marriages, both genital and psychic, is developed is that the fear of having everything taken away or of being made to look ridiculous keeps risk-taking at very safe and cautious levels. We all know cases of very attractive human beings who obviously like each other very much and who are so hung up on their fears and insecurities that they are able to move just a trifle beyond mutual psychic frigidity only occasionally. I would argue that such relationships are symbols of most human relationships, in marriage and out. Because we lack the courage to take risks, the courage to give ourselves and to accept the gift of another, we are therefore unable to take advantage of anything more than a tiny fraction of the joys, physical and psychological, that God has intended us to have in this world.

So great is the fear of risk-taking that in many relationships there is an adamant refusal to even talk about the relationship. One thinks of the woman who in her desperate need for sexual fulfillment gives a book to her husband for him to read, a book which he resolutely refuses to look at. Or, alternately, one thinks of the vast amounts of time spent in discussion of the clinical details of sexuality without any reference to the primal fears of human inadequacies which are so much more important than clinical details.

It should be obvious that friendship is only possible when passivity and activity are shared more or less equally by both partners of the relationship. One can achieve minimal stability in a relationship in which a division of labor is worked out by which one person does all the taking and the other does all the being taken. But this really represents only an atrophied relationship; in a true friendship, both the taking and the being taken dimensions of each personality ought to be free to be involved. Many marriages would be much healthier, for example, particularly in the physical but in the psychic aspects too, if the woman felt free to play the aggressive role more frequently and the man the more yielding role. But in our society, a woman can feel free to be sexually aggressive vis-à-vis her husband only when she has been previously assured of her femininity. Similarly, a man, for all the delightful fantasies he may have about what it would be like should his wife become the sexual aggressor, cannot encourage or permit such behavior unless he is reasonably confident of his own masculinity. It is striking that despite the fact that most people have extremely powerful fantasies about the pleasures to be had from breaking out of the bonds of a fixed division of sexual labor, relatively few people escape such bonds.

In both the physical and psychological spheres, then, most human marriages, and indeed most human relationships, do not go much beyond the minimal level that is necessary to keep the relationship from falling apart. The reason for this minimal development is obvious: we are all terribly afraid of risking ourselves in intimacy.

2. *Friendship is rooted in mutual attraction which must grow or it will atrophy.* Social psychologists tell us that the beginnings of all human relationships are marked by two processes. In the first both partners display their wit, charm, intelligence, admirability, strength. Both are saying to the other in effect, "See how good and great I am. Admire me!" The second process, beginning immediately after the first, is exactly the opposite. "See how little I am. Protect and take care of me. I am strong but available. You should not only be impressed by me, you should also realize that I need you." This almost simultaneous plea for admiration and care involves a simultaneous manifestation of greatness and littleness, of strength and availability. Good friends become quite skilled in manifesting to the other both strength and weakness, greatness and littleness, admirability and need. They come almost to the point of overwhelming each other with power and strength, but stop short only to collapse (literally or figuratively, depending on the relationship) into each other's arms for comfort and support. The rhythm of appealing and impressing is a subtle one, just as is the parallel rhythm of taking and being taken. It is essential that both partners participate in both sorts of activities, but it is also essential that they become sophisticated in adjusting to each other's cues. Each partner fits the rhythm of his own behavior into that of the other, neither yielding his own needs completely to the relationship nor permitting his needs to dom-

inate the relationship. A friendship is like a free-floating modern dance or a subtle jazz combo; the rhythm is always continuous and always somewhat similar, yet never quite the same. The partners know how to adjust to the other's cues and simultaneously provide the other with appropriate cues.

It is important to emphasize that this free-floating rhythm never becomes static, not at least if it is still alive. In any relationship where both partners have become confident that their adjustment problem has been solved, it is safe to say that there is little left of the relationship. When adjustment ceases, the relationship has become dull; the music has stopped; the dance has ground to a halt. Unfortunately, many people grow weary of the dance and tired of the music. Certainty, stability, and fixed, predictable patterns seem much more satisfactory than the exciting but wearing process of continuous innovation. It is time, they say, that we settle down. We have taken enough risks. It is time to be sensible now. But when a human relationship settles down it has lost its vigor and its drive. Fear, uncertainty, and insecurity have triumphed over excitement, challenge, and ingenuity.

3. *Friendship is an alternation between hiding and revelation, between keeping secrets and telling them, between mystery and blatancy.* Friendship is self-revelation and exploration; but the revelation is never complete and the exploration is never finished. There are times when we are complete mysteries to the other, and there are other times when we seem obvious and transparent. If we were mysterious all the time or blatant all the time, the other would quickly lose interest. The merely mysterious person is inaccessible and the merely blatant person has no subtlety or complexity.

In all human relationships we begin as strangers and slowly discard the protections and veils, the masks and the defenses behind which we have been hiding. But we need help from the other if we are to reveal ourselves both because we need his assurance that self-revelation is safe and because it is a delight to have him share the act by which we reveal ourselves. The delight will be transient, however, if we believe that once the veil has been dropped there will be no more mystery left in our personalities. It is the promise of friendship that at no point will there be an end of new discoveries. The goal, then, is not to reveal the total self all at once, for this is impossible; it is rather to reveal the self in such a way that the other knows ever more about us while his appetite is whetted to know more. As we drop the masks and veils of defense (a process that reveals our self not only to the other but to us too), we must insist that the other permit us to share as recipient and active agent in his own self-revelation. The mutual psychological stripping process is unlike the physical stripping, which is certainly appropriate and essential in any marriage friendship. Psychological self-revelation is not a series of discreet events following more or less the same pattern with a definite beginning and a definite end; it is rather an ongoing process which once begun must go on constantly never to end at least as long as the friendship lasts.

It follows, I think, that there must be grace and elegance in the process of self-disclosure. There is a naive kind of pop psychology, popular especially with immature people who have no toleration for either complexity or ambiguity, in which it seems necessary to learn all about the other as soon as possible on the grounds that once self-revelation is complete the relationship can really begin. One finds this crude, brutal approach to self-disclosure in certain encounter groups where the fundamental assumption seems to be that if one tells everything immediately, intimacy will be automatically assured.

But, in fact, self-revelation is not something that can be completed before friendship can begin. It is an essential component of friendship for as long as it survives. Intimacy must be developed slowly, gradually, elegantly, with the proper combination of mystery and blatancy, of caution and risk. It cannot be forced crudely, directly, roughly. It is part of the natural rhythm of friendship that there are times when we disclose to the other more than is expected and other times when we offer less than is expected. We stimulate the other's desire to know more about us yet hold back until the right time for revelation has been reached. Too much self-revelation too soon would overwhelm and repel, too little would bore. We tell enough about ourselves to keep the other interested, to make him want to come back to learn more, to encourage him; but we also wish to indicate that there is always more to be learned, that there are always new delights to be revealed on another day.

It has often seemed to me that one of the functions of fashion has always been to combine mystery with blatancy at the most obvious physical level—self-disclosure with the promise of far greater things to be revealed. The old morals books used to rant against this, but I think from our present perspective we can see that fashion—obviously within some limits of taste—plays an extremely important part in the rhythm of human relationships. Beachwear is a marvelous symbol of both mystery and blatancy. The muumuu reveals practically nothing, the bikini, practically everything. In the interaction of the two we can see the process of self-revelation neatly symbolized.

Style, grace, elegance in self-hiding and self-disclosure must continue at every stage of a relationship. When there is only blatancy, or only mystery, there is trouble. In marriage or in any human friendship in which there is nothing more to be revealed, no new delights to be discovered, no new tricks to be displayed, no new fun to be enjoyed, there is no vitality. Whoever our friend is we are always in the process of attracting and she or he is always in the process of attracting us. Simultaneously, of course, we are revealing ourselves because the friend demands to know more, and is revealing herself or himself to us because we are demanding to know more. Self-revelation, then, is not merely an active disclosure; it is a response to a demand for disclosure. We encourage the other to demand that we reveal more of ourselves, and then reveal it in response to that demand. We withhold ourselves, yet we lead the other to insist on learning more, and we are perfectly delighted to share our mysteries. We are afraid to probe into the depths of the friend's mystery, yet we find such probing powerfully attractive as the friend leads us down to them. The dance goes on, then, until one or both partners lose their nerve and the rhythm is broken. Whatever rationale is offered for breaking the rhythm, the real reason is always that one and usually both persons have decided to call things to a halt; it is too risky, too dangerous to go on.

4. *Friendship is a rhythm of conquest and surrender.* In a healthy friendship, we never completely conquer the other nor do we ever completely surrender. Once the conquest has become complete, once the surrender is over, the relationship becomes routine and monotonous. If we are absolutely sure that we possess the other, there is nothing left for us to do. We must be convinced that it is still necessary for us to work at conquering, and yet all the time have sufficient signs that our work will be successful. Simultaneously, we must demand of the other that she or he work seriously at continuing their conquest of us, while at the same time communicate to the friend that we are delighted by the efforts and that the work will be successful.

One breaks out of the bonds of loneliness, fear, and isolation by offering oneself; but the act of offering is also an act of pursuit. To make oneself available for taking is to aggressively pursue taking. We must be confident of our own attractiveness to offer ourselves. We must be convinced that we have something minimally worth taking, and we must also be confident of our own strength and power to take. We want the other for ourself, but we also want to belong to her or him. There are deep and powerful fears in our personalities that say that being conquered and conquering is not worth the effort; if it were, we would probably fail anyway. Intimacy is painful. Two human beings brush up against one another in close psychic quarters and, inevitably, conflict, friction, difficulty, and misunderstanding appear. It is not worth breaking through the barriers of the other's hostility and defensiveness. We would only be jumped if we tried. Nor is there any point in attempting to attract the other to us because he or she does not like us in the first place, and how could anyone like us? It is physically difficult for two people to live in close quarters. It is even more difficult psychologically. We want to be left alone; we want privacy; we want the lonely but safe little segment of isolation we have built for ourselves. Conquest and surrender are romantic dreams that have nothing to do with the harsh nature of the real world.

Intimacy, then, is always difficult, and when it stops being difficult it stops being intimacy. It is not easy to know which strategy is most appropriate. Is it time now to break through the other's defense with vigor and force and possess fully? Or is it time to break through defenses by subterfuge? Or do we want the other to tear aside our defense mechanisms? And how do we persuade, indeed, seduce the other to do so? These questions are not easily answered. Much less is there any answer which is always right. Routine, certainty, simplicity, established patterns simply are not possible in so complex and intricate a relationship as friendship.

The imagery that I have used in previous paragraphs has obvious physical implications, but I would insist that since man is spirit, psyche permeating body, that the language is even more pertinent when one describes the far more difficult challenge of psychic conquest and surrender. We use imagery with physical overtones because it is the only imagery we have available, but physical conquest and physical surrender are relatively simple biological exercises—at least if we wish to make them so. Virtually anyone can engage in them with a greater or lesser degree of skill. Psychic conquest and psychic surrender are much more difficult, and by no means is everyone capable of them.

Now, it may well be said that all of this is very interesting, or perhaps not so interesting, but what has it to do with theology? What does it tell us about divorce, remarriage, birth control, extra- or premarital sex? What does it say about Masters and Johnson or Gay Liberation or Dr. Reuben or *The Sex Book*? My answer is, probably nothing. I am not at all sure that it is the function of Christian theology to comment on many of these things. We probably have something pertinent to say about indissolubility, reproduction, the importance of human life, respect for the human body; but I think these are secondary considerations in a theology of sexuality. That we think them to be primary is a sign of how narrowly constrained are the perspectives of our own time. The really pertinent question to ask is what light does the Christian symbol system throw on the anxieties, the fears, and the ambiguities involved in human intimacy? This is a question that I think ought to be placed not at the end of any theology of sexuality but at its very beginning.

What I have been engaged in thus far is an exercise in Paul Tillich's theological method of correlation. One describes as best one can the ambiguities of a given human experience, and then one asks how Christian symbols illumine that experience. I have insisted that the fundamental ambiguity in marriage, friendship, and sexuality has nothing to do with divorce, birth control, or homosexuality. The real ambiguity is rooted in man's pathetic desire for unity with others and his abiding fear of unity, of his passionate delight in his own vulnerability combined with his terror of being vulnerable, in his profound enjoyment of the sweetness of being able to trust and his bitter response to the possibility of having his trust betrayed. In other words, man desperately wants friendship and love, but he is terribly afraid of taking the traumatic risk of self-exposure that is necessary for love. Shame, a conviction of his own worthlessness and unlovability tells man that the risk is not worth taking and that even if he should take it. he would be betrayed. Can the Christian symbol system make any response to this primal fear of rejection?

The act of giving oneself in friendship and particularly the act of giving oneself in a permanent genital relationship involves the basic core of one's personality and the basic conviction one has about the nature of Reality, with a capital "R." If Reality is benign or gracious, then it is ultimately safe to take and be taken because no matter what happens, a gracious Reality will protect one. If, on the other hand, Reality is malign, capricious, arbitrary, then love is a risky business and surrender bound to end in disaster. Most men hesitate somewhere between Macbeth's comment that life is a tale told by an idiot, full of sound and fury, signifying nothing and Father Teilhard's comment that there is something afoot in the universe, something that looks like gestation and birth. Hesitating as they do between a belief in graciousness and a belief in capriciousness or malignity, they can give themselves in friendship and love only part way. I would argue that he who is a Christian, that is to say, one who is fully committed with his total personality to the revelation of God as contained in his words through Jesus Christ, does not hesitate; he is on the side of Father Teilhard's interpretation. While the thought of conquest and surrender may strike terror in his heart, the terror is not strong enough to stop him. I am not saying that only the Christian is capable of friendship; but I will say that a convinced, committed Christian has a far better motivation, a far deeper rationale for friendship than anyone else. The Christian knows that the Really Real is gracious.

More than gracious. One of the most important questions to which any religious system must provide the answer is do we consider the Really Real to be accessible? Does Reality, or God, or the Gods, care about us? Can we deal with the Real? Must we appease it, must we plead with it, must we remonstrate with it, must we remind it? The Christian symbol system assures us that the Real is accessible, and it goes far beyond that when it tells us that the Ground of Being, the Ultimate, whatever we want to call it, is too accessible by far. Our God is not patiently standing by and waiting for us to offer love; he is actively and vigorously pursuing us. Our God, as I have pointed out in my book, *The Jesus Myth*, is presented to us as one who is madly in love with us. Old Yahweh wheeling and dealing in the desert, the father running down the trail to embrace the prodigal son even before he can speak his act of contrition, the mad farmer showering a full day's wage on men who hadn't even worked, Jesus forgiving the sinful woman before she even spoke her sorrow, the crazy shepherd leaving a whole flock of sheep to go find one lost, foolish one, the nutty woman searching the whole day long for a tiny coin lost in the straw floor of a Palestinian hut—these are all symbols of a God whose love for us is so strong that, by human standards at least, he would be said to be mad. Our God is a God who for some crazy reason wants to be friends with us. He wants not merely to take us for his own, (an absurd concept, surely), he also wants us to take him for our own. He is a God pathetically eager to reveal himself to us, a God who is quite ready to surrender himself to us, a God who in both the Old and New Testaments delighted in revealing himself as a lover hungering for the body of his bride.

The Christian symbols, then, say it is all right to love. "But, surely," you say, "there is nothing new or startling in that. It is scarcely a relevant revelation. Everyone knows that it is all right to love."

If everyone knows it, how come so few people do it?

Our relationships are characterized by stored-up resentments, awkward divisions of labor, frustrated dreams, vast areas which by mutual consent are never discussed, trade-offs by which certain defense mechanisms of both partners are inviolable, subtle aggressions and manipulations, and brave pretenses to the outside world that all is well between us.

This is the love by which all men shall know that we are followers of Jesus?

The revelation of Jesus tells us that we can move beyond such stalemates and break out of the rigidities which keep our joys and pleasures at such a low level. I think most of us understand implicitly that this is the message of Jesus, but we do not want to believe it because if we do, a profound revolution in our lives will have to occur. We will have to transform ourselves (or "repent" as the scripture used to translate the word *metanein*). And no one wants to do that.

Much better that we argue about celibacy, birth control, abortion, infallibility, Norman Mailer, Germaine Greer—all the really important issues.

If we reject the Christian imagery of God, let us reject it for the right reasons. Let us dismiss it because it is absurd or blasphemous or too good to be true or disgraceful or embarrassing. Let us not reject it because of papal infallibility or birth control or *Humanae Vitae* or clerical celibacy or pop versions of Sigmund Freud or clichés quoted from the counterculture and self-proclaimed radicals. Father Schillebeeckx has said that Christianity is the revelation that humanity is possible. I would go further and say that Christianity is the revelation that friendship and love are possible, that we are free to love, that man need not be afraid to give himself over to friendship, to take and be taken. For if the Really Real, the Absolute Ground of Being, *ipsum esse*, proclaims itself as a friend, then the whole universe is out to do us good. The joys of human friendship turn out merely to be an anticipation of the great life of friendship and joy prepared for us by this splendid, dizzying, crazy God of ours, whose Word made flesh manifested himself to us in these incredible words: "Behold, I do not call you servants; I call you friends."

2

Sexuality as Hunger

In a certain Catholic parish not so long ago a layman was given the opportunity of preaching the Sunday homily. (I dare say no one consulted the other laity as to whether they wanted to hear a lay preacher at all much less this particular one.) A clinical psychologist and (heaven save us) a marriage counselor, this layman devoted part of his "homily" to quoting statistics that proved (a) there was no evidence that premarital intercourse had any negative effect on marriage adjustment, and (b) there was no evidence to support the frequently heard contention that those who failed in their first marriages were very likely to fail in their second. For some unaccountable reason the parishioners who heard this "homily" were more than a little offended by it.

Leaving aside the question of whether it is in good taste for Catholic scholars to use the Sunday pulpit as a means of shocking the laity who are not as sophisticated as they, there remains the question of whether the empirical data the psychologist quoted has any real pertinence to the discussion of values for sexuality in marriage.

Much of his data, I think, would be greeted with raised eyebrows by professional researchers who would want to know where the study was done, who did it, what kinds of questions were asked, and, especially, what kind of sample was involved. (In many articles purporting to provide information about the "sexual revolution," it turns out that the data are based on research done in college counseling clinics—scarcely a random sample of the American people.) One might also wonder about the theoretical assumptions underlying his presentation. Anyone who has paid much attention to the literature on marriage adjustment knows that the strongest predictor—frequently about the only one that matters—of marital adjustment is whether the two parties grew up in a family where the relationship between husband and wife was basically healthy and happy. If the man and woman are from such families the odds on a satisfactory marriage adjustment of their own are very high. On the other hand, if both of them are from relatively unsatisfactory family backgrounds, it can be reasonably expected that they will have a very difficult time working out a satisfactory relationship. Premarital sexuality may very well be an "intervening" variable between family background and marriage adjustment. It may indicate a childish or exploitive approach to sex which one learned in one's family or origin and will practice in one's own family. It is the immaturity of the exploitiveness that will disrupt the marriage and not the premarital intercourse, which may or may not have been a sign of immaturity and exploitiveness.

But most important of all, one does not arrive at sexual values by counting noses. Even if it turned out that every remarriage after divorce led to very high levels of marital satisfaction, this finding by itself would say nothing about the desirability of divorce; nor would a strong positive relationship between premarital intercourse and marriage adjustment settle the question of the morality of premarital intercourse. I will yield to no man in my respect for the ability of survey research to provide useful and important information for decision making, but survey research is no solution to moral and ethical questions. Ultimately our values depend neither on what everyone does nor on rather narrow statistical measures of whether something "works" or not but on our view of the nature of man and of human relationships. Empirical research certainly provides input for information of our ethical wisdom (another name for our views of the nature of man and his relationships), but anyone who works professionally with the tools of survey research knows how inadequate they are even to address the fundamentally empirical problems which are their legitimate area. As the principal norm for ethical wisdom, survey research is about as appropriate as first-grade arithmetic would be for dealing with astrophysics.

But there is an implicit assumption in much of the popular and semiserious literature that attempts to derive a sexual ethics from the Kinsey report or its more sophisticated successors, and that assumption is the strange notion that "modern man" is the only intelligent and enlightened people that ever lived. We are the first members of the human species who have been sexually "liberated," at least in any considerable numbers. Everything that was said in the matter of human sexuality before Jung and Freud is irrelevant. There is nothing to be learned from the past, and our only appropriate stance vis-a-vis the wisdom of the past on human sexuality is to liberate ourselves from its rigid superstitious norms and from the guilt feelings that those norms impose. Our predecessors were ignorant, unenlightened, uninformed, stupid. There is nothing to be learned from them; we can only learn from our own contemporaries. Therefore, we take surveys to find out what our contemporaries are doing and decide that whatever the majority are doing is moral. If only we can free ourselves completely from the nagging scruples which say that maybe, just maybe, there is something to be said for the old prohibitions, we would become sexually free and all our "hangups" would disappear.

I fear that this "temporal ethnocentrism" is widespread, particularly in the half-educated segment of our population, that is, the segment that thinks the shallow half-truths served up in the college lecture room or counseling center really represent wisdom. It is terribly difficult to discuss sexuality with this substantial component of the American population and not run up against the stone wall of the assumption that we are enlightened about sex and our narrow, rigid, prohibitive ancestors were not.

I am not attempting to defend the traditional sexual wisdom; it certainly had its limitations and inadequacies. Much less am I prepared to defend the rigid norms that attempted to specify this wisdom for concrete situations (but frequently in fact distorted it). The legalism of the moral theology books, the catechisms, the confessional—and the legalism of primitive tribal codes in non-Christian cultures, for that matter—is rarely an adequate expression of ethical wisdom, though the human race even today is hard put to make do without codes. But what I do insist on is that the norms of the past deserve to be understood on their own terms and from "the inside." The casual dismissal of traditional wisdom with cheap arguments (such as "the only reason for indissolubility is to provide care for the children") or bad statistics is not a sign of enlightenment but rather of superficiality and immaturity. Thus, as a social scientist analyzing the nature of human relationships and of human friendship—as described in the last chapter —I am convinced that there is a strain toward permanence in human relationships. I therefore think it is stupid to refuse to examine the almost universal human wisdom on the subject of the permanency of the marriage relationship to discover whether it may possibly speak to some aspects of the human condition which we arrogant and supremely self-confident moderns may have missed. Mind you, to say that there is a "strain toward permanence" in sexual relationships does not necessarily commit one to the present requirements of the code of canon law, but one should examine the possibility that the code is trying to cope, however ineptly and inadequately, with what is a very real human dilemma.

This is not a book about indissolubility, birth control, abortion, homosexuality, extramarital intercourse, transvestism, spouse swapping, or bestiality, and I do not propose to be sidetracked into a discussion of any of these essentially peripheral issues. But I do wish to assert that those who equate traditional human wisdom with specific answers on these questions merely display their own lack of wisdom and sophistication.

The most fundamental insight that primitive man had about sexuality is one that we frequently overlook or forget: that it is a raw, primal, basic power over which we have only very limited control. Primitive man invariably viewed sexuality as sacred, because for him the "sacred" was the "powerful," and sexuality was one of the fundamental forces that kept the universe going. We have "prettied up" sexuality with thousands of years of civilized conventions and now we have rationalized it by the use of glib psychotherapeutic terminology, hence deceiving ourselves into thinking calm, cool, casual discussion is a meaningful and effective way of coping with our sexual drives. Ancient man knew better.

The most ancient human works of art that we have discovered are figurines unearthed from the ruins of human communities that existed in Siberia 30,000 years ago. They are simultaneously sexual and religious. Primitive man knew his life depended on the fertility of the fields and of animals, that if the crops failed or the herds did not reproduce he would die. He also knew the continuation of his tribe depended on human fertility. Since fertility and life were so closely connected and since life was something sacred, fertility was sacred too. But ancient man also knew what tremendous power his own sexuality had over his own behavior. He was afraid of that power because he knew that it could drive him into a frenzy. He did not understand it, he could not contain it, and therefore, like every other power that was both strong and mysterious, his own sexuality became something sacred.

The incredible variety of sexual taboos that primitive man devised represented an attempt, frequently misguided and occasionally bizarre, to contain that raw, primal force so that it would not disrupt the fragile relationships that bound him together with the other members of his village or his clan. Modern man may dismiss human concern about sexuality as "guilt hangups" and he may argue that sex can be "casual," but in fact the only reason some modern men can practice what they think is casual sex is that society has built up elaborate structures of conventionality which enable it to more or less effectively prevent untamed sexuality from tearing it apart. What is called "casual" sex really isn't casual at all. It involves the violation of some sexual conventions within the protective context created by other sexual conventions. One need only see the movie *The Clockwork Orange* to know what human society would be like if a sufficiently large number of its members decided to practice really casual sex. The result would be anarchy, with the fabric of society coming apart as more and more of us took possession of any readily available sexual partner.

Our ancestors may not have understood many things about sexuality (it is just possible that there are many things that we don't understand either). Their conventions may have been ill-advised, counterproductive, and harmful to the individual person; furthermore, many of the conventions may have deteriorated into hard, rigid legalisms which no longer serve the function for which they came into being, but at least they understood what many of us apparently do not: the rational, casual, "chatty" approach to sexuality as exemplified in Dr. Reuben's book, *Everything You Always Wanted to Know about Sex, but Were Afraid to Ask,* is simply inadequate to cope with such a raw, basic human hunger. In the absence of strong conventions untamed sexuality will destroy human society. The ancients knew this; we apparently do not know it. In this respect, they were much wiser than we are.

And yet every one of us experiences our own sexuality as imperious and demanding. Our craving for sexual satisfaction, for sexual relief, for sexual union permeates our being and frequently dominates our behavior to the exclusion of all else. One man put it to me quite simply, "When I am traveling, if my wife isn't with me I end up either chasing waitresses or punching bartenders." Those who delight in the rational, casual vocabulary of Dr. Reuben will be offended by such a blunt, earthy description of the sexual drive. They will forget, or try to forget, that their own sexual hunger has frequently led them, if not exactly to chase waitresses or punch bartenders, to come close to very similar behavior. Our sexual hunger frequently tells us to do things which appall our more rational and civilized personality dimensions. Our hunger for sexual satisfaction is probably not as powerful as our hunger for food, but then few of us in contemporary America are hungry for food for long periods of time. We are able to cope with that hunger by eating three times a day. Satisfaction of our sexual appetites is not nearly so easily accomplished.

Because our sexual hunger is so powerful and so pervasive, it becomes involved with every strange and bizarre trait in our personalities. There is not a single neurotic defense mechanism that we've developed which is not at least partially sexual in origin and partially sexual in its manifestations. Our defense mechanisms exist to protect our own fears of sexual inadequacy; and we impose neurotic behavior on others as a form of sexual aggression, which substitutes, though just barely, for more obvious and more explicit sexuality. Even the most mature of us (and who is all that mature?) has severe problems preventing his sexual hunger from disrupting his life and destroying his values. Sexuality is a raw elemental force which sweeps us along like a thirty-five-mile-an-hour wind would toss a tiny sailboat on the waters of Lake Michigan. Any approach to understanding and living with sexuality that does not take into account the immense and undifferentiated power of sexual passion is naive and self-defeating.

Anyone may read Dr. Reuben's book and now know all the answers to all the questions he used to be afraid to ask, but his sexual hunger remains untamed. The body of a sexual partner, only remotely available—fully clad in the next room, perhaps—or existing only in fantasy, can intervene and instantly sweep away the most serious thoughts, the most important activities, the most lofty aspirations, the most critical responsibilities and demand response *now*. One may wake up in the morning with a long and busy agenda for our day's activities, only to discover that he or she feels an insistent demand for the body of a person of the opposite sex. The day is doomed to be a struggle between the agenda of responsibilities and the paralyzing longing which the sex demand insidiously interjects into every thought and action. The conventions of society and the controls his sense of responsibility exert will probably get him through the day with the agenda discharged in some fashion or other, but he must admit honestly to himself that if he could have suspended or appeased his sexual hunger, he would have done a much better job on the agenda.

Even though the experience I have described in the last paragraph is widespread, many still blind themselves to it and argue that the only real sexual problem is guilt feelings inherited from childhood experiences and inflexible religious norms. Guilt may mess up our sexuality, but even a man totally free from neurotic guilt must admit, if he is honest, that the reduction of guilt feelings does not contribute very much to the taming of the sexual tiger.

Not that the taming of sexuality is an appropriate goal, for a tame sexuality is not a human sexuality—and probably one that is not much fun either. To argue, as I have in these pages, that sexuality is a raw, elemental force is not to say that one should be ashamed of primitive passion, much less try to tame it. The argument, rather, is that the beginning of sexual wisdom is to understand that we are dealing with a power that cannot be tamed. Living with sexuality does not mean eliminating its primal force; it means, rather, understanding how primal the force is and channeling it in directions which are both socially and personally productive.

We are frequently informed that ours is becoming a more "permissive" society in which the atmosphere is much more permeated by sexuality than it has been in the past. Observers dispute whether this is a good thing or a bad thing. The availability of pornographic literature, the use of the naked human form (usually female) as an advertising gimmick, the appearance of "16mm films from San Francisco" in neighborhood theaters—these are praised by the liberals as a sign that we are becoming more like Sweden and Denmark and damned by conservatives on the ground that we are becoming more like Babylon. (I can't really believe that the liberal defenders of pornography think that the "sex shops" of Copenhagen represent maturity, liberation or happiness, but to each his own, I guess.) But much of this is nonsense. What makes our world pervasively sexual is not the presence of more or less unclad bodies of the opposite sex, but rather the very presence of bodies of the opposite sex (for that matter, as no one is completely heterosexual, bodies of our own sex too), no matter how covered with clothes they may be. The blatant sexuality of this society, for example, did not arise from the fact that an occasional woman—or indeed, perhaps many women—may appear on the streets braless in a transparent blouse. The real sexuality of the social atmosphere comes from the fact that there are women at all and that they have breasts—no matter how they cover them. However breasts are hidden or displayed is much less important than the fact that the man *knows* that they are there and that therefore this other human being he encounters (even if it is only a transitory meeting on the elevator of his office building) is a potential sexual partner. That is the *real* problem. Any man has powerful sexual hungers, and this woman standing next to him, even for a fleeting moment, is capable of alleviating these hungers, at least temporarily. Of course she, too, has powerful sexual hungers, though she may be less willing to admit them to herself. She, too, realizes that this man next to her on the elevator can provide her with some moments of intense pleasure. The two of them are disciplined, more or less adequately, by social conventions and personal responsibility. He is not likely to rape her, nor is she likely to seduce him, but both know that intercourse between the two of them is a radical biological possibility and one that promises immense delight. The encounter may be brief, the sexual overtones are implicit and perhaps largely unconscious, the latent power is sufficiently well chained that it will not be released; yet, it is there, stirring round the depths of both personalities.

Let us add to this elevator scene elements that are supposed to be part of our uniquely "permissive" modern situation. Let us assume that the elevator is going from the swimming pool to the fifth floor. Let us further assume that the woman is taking the birth control pill and has no fear of pregnancy. Let us also assume that neither of the two considers himself or herself bound by the old morality "hangups." Finally, let us assume that they are both clad in swimming pool garb, the blatant sexuality of which is somewhat diffused by the openness of the swimming pool environment, but which is greatly enhanced by the close, intimate quarters of the elevator.

These changed circumstances may increase somewhat the possibility of rape and/or seduction—but not very much. They may increase the mutual awareness of sexual electricity between them. By the very fact that the clothes leave so little to the imagination, fantasy may begin to work at a more active and explicit fashion than it might otherwise. In fact, the changed circumstances only modify slightly the fundamental physical and psychological fact of the situation. Both bodies know and both persons know, however subconsciously, that they are alone with someone who could fulfill their sexual hungers. Such an encounter in any society, however permissive or restrictive, is fundamentally the same experience. The surrounding attitudes and customs modify only slightly the primal forces that are at work in such an encounter.

In other words, if we are to live with our sexuality, we must begin by understanding that its problems and its possibilities, its hungers and its satisfactions, are part of the human condition quite independent of particular time and space. There are both problems and opportunities in our own time that are unique, but they only modify and perhaps enhance the elementary human passions that are involved.

Let us illustrate this with another example. A young man sits on the beach, staring dreamily at the water (as young men do when there's nothing better to stare at). A particularly well-proportioned young woman crosses his field of vision clad in the skimpiest of bikinis. Without the young man's having to issue any instructions, his imagination disposes of the bra and the panties, and he enjoys in fantasy the splendors of the girl's unclad body. Behind him sits the Puritan. Assuming that he represents the right wing of that movement, we know that he is shocked at what is going on. The girl is a shameless hussy for displaying herself in such a manner! The young man is a dirty-minded punk for thinking what he is thinking! In other times, when people had a sense of decency, such foul things wouldn't occur! (Right-wing Puritans always think in exclamations.) If the Puritan is left-wing, he will rejoice that in our more progressive day the standards of beachwear are such that young people can enjoy the transient seduction fantasies that were not available to them in the past. (It is worth noting that both the Puritan of the right and the Puritan of the left are also enjoying the young woman's body, but from the secure perspective of moralizing about the young man.)

But both Puritans are kidding themselves. The clock could be rolled back to 1890 and the young woman be covered from neck to toe in the beachwear of that day. It wouldn't matter much. The young man would see her in a socially legitimated form of undress and his imagination would still perform exactly the same operations as would his descendant's in 1970. There would be more clothes for his fantasy to strip away, but the process would be just as quick. In neither case would he be "dirty-minded," though in both cases, he might feel guilty about his fantasy. He would simply be a male of the human race who suddenly experiences the presence of a potential sexual partner arrayed in the fashion which indicates availability somewhat more than does ordinary street garb. The impact on him, be it in 1890 or 1973, is not unlike being hit over the head with a club.

And in both instances it is safe to presume that the young woman knows that she is in a situation where it is more socially acceptable for her to make her body available for inspection by members of the opposite sex. Both in 1890 and in 1973, she may hesitate about doing this, but she has a powerful need to make men look at and admire her body and so overcomes her hesitation. She, at the same time, has a need to look at and admire the bodies of young men. Whether it be a three-ring bikini or the bathing dress of 1890 is less important than the explicit statement, which we permit on the beach but not on the street, that here is a body which may be available to satisfy my body on the condition that I make my body available to satisfy yours.

As long as there have been young men and women, such encounters have occurred (though not necessarily on the beach), and as long as there will be young men and young women, such encounters will continue to happen. There is a good deal more to falling in love, however, and much, much more to preparing for marriage than such primitive and basic displays of masculinity and femininity. But the powerful if transient mutual desire of the beach encounter represents the radical roots of human sexuality. No matter how sophisticated or how mature or how self-possessed or how casual or how cool we may think our approach to sexuality is, we are all of us basically boys and girls at the beach.

I am not suggesting that these primal sexual responses dominate every encounter between a man and a woman, or that they are the only important thing in the encounter, or that indeed they need have much in the way of a direct effect on the substantive purpose which has brought them together. Thus, if a man and a woman are working together, there is certainly no biological determination that demands that they sleep with each other or that their sexuality ever need to be discussed explicitly or that there will be any problem in their working together constructively. On the contrary, they may be able to work together more effectively than colleagues of the same sex. I am saying that their sexual hungers are present, their sexual fantasies are at work, their sexual awareness will be active, and they will be kidding themselves if they think that their sexual differences do not have a powerful if subtle influence on the relationship that emerges between them. Their relationship may go far beyond these fantasies and develop in directions that have nothing to do with them; but as members of the human race they must face the fact that such fantasies create part of the fundamental substratum of their relationship, a substratum that may be much more obvious and important in some relationships than in others, but which is never, repeat never, totally absent.

Civilization developed a set of conventions very early in the game that limited the sexual fantasies of most of us to the imagination. Society simply would not survive and hence cannot tolerate a situation in which everyone is free to act on his sexual fantasies. In Norman O. Brown's polymorphously perverse society, not only would nothing ever get done, we probably would end up killing one another. Men and women do not casually rape each other on the streets (and that is the only kind of sex which would really be casual). We have all learned to restrain *that* kind of sexual impulse (or at least most of us have). That is the only sort of sexual liberation that is complete liberation. Any compromise with it indicates that we do acknowledge in fact that some sorts of convention and restraint have to be imposed on the imperious demands of sexual hunger.

Many societies, and not necessarily primitive ones

either, recognize the immense tensions that sexual self-restraint impose. They compensate for the tension by designating certain times of the year as periods when "anything goes" sexually, when citizens are free to act out if not all their sexual fantasies at least to surrender to many of their normally restrained impulses. The Saturnalia in Rome, the medieval carnival and Mardi gras (of which the modern ones are pale imitations), and the American New Year's Eve orgy are all times when some of the restraints are temporarily lowered. It is interesting to note, incidentally, that many of these periods of casual sex were like the beginnings of new years in that new life, born in the midst of a concession to the demanding and sacred power of human fertility.

There are obviously both Christian and humanistic objections to periodic orgies and to the permanent semi-orgy of spouse swapping (or "swinging," as it is called in American suburbia). But societies that tolerate and encourage such behavior have discovered an important point; that is, some release is needed for the tensions that build up when sexual fantasies are limited to the imagination. Those value systems which, quite properly in my judgment, object to orgies and to "swinging" must devise alternative measures to achieve the same purpose. Presumably, such measures would have to consist of periodic modifications of the relationship between husband and wife in which some of the tensions that build up by the normal restraints imposed by fidelity and the ordinary pattern of their relationship one with another can be released. The solution will most likely involve a development of a relationship between a husband and wife in which their respective fantasies can be more adequately expressed with each other at certain times. Obviously, this is an area which must be explored more fully, and it should be with an awareness that the orgy had an important social function for which a Christian and humanist alternative must be found. Minimally, every husband and wife should understand that if they expect fidelity, they must not only tolerate but encourage a sexual relationship in which both their fantasies enjoy considerable freedom to frolic and experiment. Variety seems to be a fundamental part of human sexual hunger. If one does not find it in the marriage bed—or whatever substitutes fantasy may devise—one will be under strong pressure to look for it elsewhere. The pressure is not, of course, irresistible; no one is biologically determined to be unfaithful. However, this book is not concerned with the inevitability of sin but rather with the power of human passion.

To put the matter somewhat differently, a woman who is learning to live with both her own sexuality and her husband's recognizes the fact that he is a sexual being and that every woman, particularly every reasonably attractive woman, is a potential sexual partner. The wife must understand that it is necessary for the health of their marriage for him to believe that, all things considered, no other woman can provide him with more sexual excitement than she can.

Similarly, a man must admit to himself—and it will probably be much harder for him to do so—that his wife must sometimes yearn, in the depths of her fantasies to have her body powerfully and demandingly caressed by other men. He therefore knows that the health of their marriage requires that his wife realize that, all things considered, no other man can challenge and satisfy her sexually as well as her husband can.

I am not attempting to prescribe tactics to guarantee marital fidelity. My point is that dull sex is not an adequate response to the profound and tempestuous power of sexuality found within men and women, and both husband and wife should understand that.

But even in a genitally satisfying marriage not all sexual energies are drained away. Those who are not married have even more free-floating sexual energy than those who are. Celibate or married, however, some if not all of our sexual energy will be diverted into other channels. Nongenital friendships, aggression, ambition, artistic creativity, altruism, idealism, social commitment are all forms of human behavior which, while they may or may not be sexual in their origins, certainly become sexual in their manifestations because of their capacity to absorb diverted sexual energy. Everybody either sublimates or represses some sexual energy. Living with sexuality involves not merely the diversion of sexual energy but understanding how and why we divert it and exercising sufficient control over the diversion so that the result is not harmful to us or to others. Much of the punishment we impose on ourselves and our friends and families is the result of poorly understood and badly diverted sexual energy. Indeed, even in the sexual relationship itself, energy can be diverted in such a way as to threaten if not destroy the relationship.

Let us examine the problem of the diversion and misdirection of sexual energy in a marriage relationship.

The most obvious thing that can be said about sexual hunger and marriage is that in marriage one has the body of a member of the opposite sex directly and immediately available. There are no legal or moral norms preventing one from taking that body whenever he (or she) is hungry for it. Society condones obtaining satisfaction from this other body, and society tells the other that he (or she) is expected to respond with delight when pleasure is demanded from him (or her).

Furthermore, as time goes on the partners begin to know each other's physiological secrets. A man learns not merely how to arouse a woman but how to arouse *this* woman, or a woman understands not merely what a man's weaknesses are but the weaknesses of *this* man. Also, they have experienced repeatedly the highly pleasurable satisfaction of their hunger through sexual intercourse with each other. Like every other thing a human being enjoys, this satisfaction creates a predisposition for more satisfaction—not merely more generalized sexual satisfaction, but the highly specific, particularized satisfaction that *this* partner can provide. They also realize that assuaging their sexual hunger by making love to their spouse takes a good deal of tension out of other relationships. Direct sexual tension and diverted sexual tension becomes anger or aggressiveness or bitchiness.

Finally, and most importantly, of course, intercourse is the natural expression of the interpersonal and fully human love that a husband and wife expect to experience with each other and which they both believe is at the core of their marriage. With all of these factors at work it would seem that it would be extremely difficult for a man and wife not to be sexually aroused vis-à-vis each other much of the time. Indeed, one would expect that two such people might even have a hard time keeping their hands off one another even in public. Everything in their relationship would seem to be straining toward a constant mutual satisfaction of sexual hunger.

But there are other factors at work that not only change the situation but sometimes reverse it completely. First of all, one simply cannot spend all one's time making love. Both husband and wife have other obligations and other responsibilities. They must exercise some sort of restraint if only because other things in life demand their attention and also because a life together in which there was nothing but genitality would eventually become dull. Let us concede that most American couples could probably spend more time on their physical relationship than they actually do. Married sex is too often hurried, episodic, and lacking in elegance and grace. But even if more time could be spent, it is still true that some restraints would have to be imposed. Not all of one's life can be given over to genitality.

Furthermore, there is a need for sexual privacy. One might question whether privacy might have become obsessive in American society, thus generating equally obsessive spurning of all privacy in the communes and in certain sensitivity groups. It might be much healthier for husband and wife and for their children if there was more room for them to display their passion and affection for one another in other places besides the bedroom. However, intercourse is still a private act and a desire for privacy may well be a normal aspect of the human condition.

Thus both the requirements of other obligations and of privacy impose even on a husband and wife some limitations of the freedom they enjoy in the satisfaction of sexual hungers. But these limitations—essentially limitations of the external world—are minor compared to those that arise from the fears, anxieties, defense mechanisms and resentments out of the past and the present which focus on the marriage bed. The need to "get even," the need to punish, the need to protect and defend, the need to keep others at bay all impose immense constraints on married sexuality and divert sexual hunger into self-destructive and punitive paths. I remember an incident which illustrates the pathos of such defensiveness and punitiveness with a special vigor because it has to do explicitly with that symbol of the marriage union, the nuptial bed.

A group of young people I knew were spending several days at a summer resort area. Some of the couples were married, others, a bit younger, were at various stages of courtship and engagement. One night a number of couples were sitting around talking. The only couple in this particular group that was married began to urge their younger friends to think seriously about ordering twin beds when they began to buy furniture for their future homes. For, as the wife pointed out, even though a double bed may look very attractive before marriage, it is a great inconvenience afterwards.

The younger people listened in disbelief. Both the man and his wife were magnificent physical specimens. By all physical and apparent personal dimensions, the couple seemed made for each other. The younger people could not believe that the two of them did not crave the closest possible physical intimacy. Nor could they believe that in their own marriages they could possibly let their spouse have another bed.

In part, what the married couple was saying was merely a statement of sober realism. Sharing a bed with someone else means conceding a considerable amount of convenience and privacy. It is awkward, uncomfortable, and frequently friction-producing. It only becomes tolerable when there is a tremendous physical and emotional payoff in such close intimacy. The marriage bed in a way symbolizes the ambiguity of marriage: the sexual passions of husband and wife have absorbed them into a relationship which is both physically and psychologically inconvenient and quite frequently abrasive.

The young married couple, perhaps without realizing it (or perhaps with deliberate intent to punish one another), were saying in effect that in their marriage, the powers of repulsion were presently much stronger than those of attraction. They really couldn't stand to sleep side by side and the presence of the other's body next to them at night, far from producing delight, was in fact causing disgust.

What precisely had happened is beyond the scope of this booklet, but the feelings are common enough, even if their expression is less so. In the battle between delight and disgust, our fears, our resentments, our immaturity frequently load the dice in favor of disgust. But our sexual hungers and energies are not thereby eliminated. On the contrary, they are diverted toward reinforcing the hatred and the disgust. Two men or two women who must temporarily share very cramped physical quarters may fall back on old sibling rivalries out of the past to give shape and form to the friction and resentment that builds up in their physical environment. But since there is no (or very little) sexual frustration and disappointment in their relationship, only a minor amount of frustrated sexual energy is being diverted into reinforcing their friction. The marriage situation, however, is totally different. Because the whole thing is about sexual pleasure and satisfaction, both husband and wife feel cheated that their expectations are not being met, and resentment opens wide the floodgates through which sexual energy passes to be converted into resentment and disgust, which in its turn leads to even more sexual frustration. A vicious circle has set in which will not necessarily lead either to the divorce court or infidelity but will most certainly result in the extinction of sexual passion. And still the extinction of sexual passion will not lead to the elimination of sexual energy. It merely means that a substantial component of sexual hunger is now going to be devoted to blaming, hurting, and, when possible, punishing the other for what he or she has done. It is not merely that the couple will move into separate beds (and later into separate bedrooms); now they will devote a considerable amount of their lives—and not always unconsciously either—to punishing one another. They no longer have to restrain outbreaks of sexuality, they have to work themselves up to having intercourse at all. What could easily have been an extremely satisfying outlet for sexual hunger has not only failed to be satisfying but has notably increased the frustration and tension in the lives of both spouses.

One cannot readily dispose of a source of sexual satisfaction that has been blighted by resentment and disgust. The body of the other is still there. Part of the personality still longs for it while another part may experience nothing but revulsion at the thought of union. One is trapped, then, in a situation in which there is not only little satisfaction but in which there is ever increasing dissatisfaction, frustration, disgust, resentment, anger, and hatred. In such a situation infidelity is less a direct outlet for sexual hunger than it is an indirect outlet, which finds its real satisfaction in punishing the other.

There is no need to turn to Dr. Reuben for a catalog of all the sick forms of sexual aberrations. One need only look at a marriage in which disgust has triumphed over delight to see how brutal and punitive the sexual drive can be when it is diverted into neurotic channels. Two people whose bodies once ached for each other (and, presumably, still do to some extent) are busily engaged in an attempt to slowly and painfully destroy each other because their longing got sidetracked. They are not only not in possession of their sexuality (few really are), they have let it get completely out of control. In many cases they are not only not capable of passion for one another (save intermittantly, perhaps), they are really not capable of passion with anyone, because so much of their libidos have been directed toward hatred, resentment, and disgust.

A marriage in which sexual hunger is displaced by resentment and punitiveness is but the classic example of how we can divert the primal life force of sexuality into self-destructive behaviors. One does not have to go far beyond the two rigid bodies juxtaposed in the disgust-filled marriage bed to find the corrupt businessman or politician getting his kicks out of amassing money; the viciously aggressive lawyer stopping at nothing to win a case, steal a client, or cut down a colleague; the neurotic housewife who turns her children into misfits; or the suburban gossip-monger who delights in destroying another's personality. All these behaviors are clearly a result of the diversion of sexual energy and are at least a probable sign of a frustrated and unhappy marriage.

I do not know what happened to the young people who advised their friends to invest in twin beds. They were in a very difficult and painful time of their marriage. Their relationship could go either way. Disgust or delight could win. They could go on to separate bedrooms and separate lives. But if that is the way they went, God help them—and God forgive them, too. I believe that God did not want them to have separate beds or separate lives, for he made them in such a way that where they really belonged was in passionate embrace with each other just as often as they could possibly find the opportunity, delighting in each other's bodies and being swept along by the primal passion of their mutual hunger. To turn away from the imperious joys of such an embrace denies not so much their marriage vows as the fact of their creation as sexual beings.

Yet even a happy acceptance of one's sexuality leaves a considerable amount of surplus sexual energy unexpended. The advantage of having a healthy genital relationship is that there is much greater likelihood of one's excess sexual energy being devoted to constructive, healthy, creative activities rather than to self-destruction and self-punishment. Those who for one reason or another find themselves in the celibate state must understand that the difference between them and married people is not that they must sublimate while married people do not have to, but simply that the celibate has somewhat more sexual energy to devote to other activities. According to the ancient law of the grass being greener in someone else's yard, the celibate would be inclined to greatly underestimate the amount of sublimation required of the married person. Marriage is obviously something of a response to sexual hunger. Even the most satisfying genital relationship by no means eliminates all the free-floating sexual energy and hunger that possesses one. There is plenty of sexual hunger and emotional tension in the lives of a husband and wife despite their fundamentally happy marriage. The celibate who thinks that marriage eliminates sexual hunger simply doesn't know what goes on in the world.

The celibate must come to terms with the fact that he or she is a sexual being. The celibate's fantasy evaluates members of the opposite sex as potential partners every bit as automatically as does everyone else's. He can no more prevent such fantasizing than can anyone else. He attempts to persuade himself that that electric sexual tension in the elevator doesn't exist or that he doesn't yearn to caress the body of the person sitting next to him on the airplane. He is merely kidding himself; worse still, he is engaging in extremely neurotic repression. The celibate may be well advised to impose limitations on his fantasy (and, of course, married people know that they must limit their fantasy lives too—if they are ever going to get anything done). But restraining fantasy does not mean eliminating it, and renouncing genitality for one reason or another does not mean either that one ceases to have sexual hungers or that one is immune from appraising members of the opposite sex as potential genital partners.

The celibate, male or female, has made a decision, hopefully for good and mature reasons, to engage in more diversion of sexual energies than the married person must attempt. In one sense, this makes his sexual posture radically different from that of the married person, but in another sense, restraint, discipline, self-control, and sublimation are part of the human condition and the celibate misses the whole point if he thinks he is the only one who must practice them—or even that it is appreciably easier for a married person than it is for him.

My purpose in this volume is not to defend either the possibility or the desirability of celibacy as an option for certain kinds of committed persons. Obviously, I believe it is both feasible and in some cases admirable; but that is another question perhaps to be discussed in another book. My only point here is that celibates do not cease to be sexual and they have no monopoly on sublimation.

Recently, many people have raised the question about friendships that are "erotic" but not genital. (In the perspective of this booklet, of course, all relationships between a man and a woman, or indeed between any two human beings, have an erotic component. The couple riding from the swimming pool to the fifth floor are in a very erotic, if silent and transient, certainly nongenital, relationship.) The word "erotic" is used by people who are concerned about these kinds of friendships in the sense that two people who are not married to each other become very close friends and permit certain kinds of pleasure. They share powerful affection and psychological intimacy with perhaps some sorts of physical intimacy not intended to lead to genital relationships—a kind of behavior which indeed explicitly excludes genitality from the relationship. They may claim the right to kiss, embrace, caress, and even, perhaps, to partially undress one another.

The question is most frequently raised by priests and nuns who wonder whether some forms of psychological and physical intimacy are compatible with the celibate commitment—or perhaps may even reinforce it. But the questions are also raised by married people who may be repelled by the promiscuity of "swinging" but nevertheless wonder whether close friendships can be strongly erotic and still compatible with the marriage bond.

There is a good deal of cynical leering about such relationships both among the unsophisticated, whose notions of sexuality never get beyond locker-room humor, and among the highly sophisticated, who might think that "swinging" is a healthy form of "sexual outlet" and that "incomplete" relationships are frustrating and unhealthy. On both sides there is the conviction that it is not only impossible but somehow or another unnatural to engage in the exchange of physical affection—at least of the passionate variety—while excluding intercourse as the "natural" end of such affection. Herbert Richardson in his recent book *Nun, Witch, Playmate* vigorously denounces such a perspective and argues that the medieval advocates of courtly love, who believed in intimacy without intercourse, really understood much more about the polymorphous nature of human love than do modern "genital determinists." Arguing against Harvey Cox, Richardson contends that adolescent "petting," far from being a sick and frustrating manifestation of "incomplete sexuality" is in fact part of the healthy experience of growing in physical and psychological sexual sensitivity. Such petting represents a development in the ability to give and to receive affection; it need not be ordered toward proximate genital intercourse. Richardson does not say so explicitly, but there is obviously implicit in his argument the possibility that for married people, "petting-like" behavior with another can be expression of deep, serious affection, which is neither false nor incomplete because intercourse is excluded as anything but a radical possibility and which need not represent a threat to the marriage commitment. (For a fictional account of the multiple loves of man, see Gabriel Fielding's remarkable book, *Gentlemen in Their Season*.)

I report Richardson's position, as I understand it, not because I wish to endorse it but because it seems to me that, at least in his argument with Harvey Cox, he has by far the better of the discussion.

But quite apart from Richardson, what is to be said about "incomplete" erotic relationships? The only response I am capable of giving is that I don't know. On the theoretical level it seems to me possible that an argument can be made in favor of the feasibility of such relationships. On the practical level, I see all kinds of difficulties and problems, if only because I am not sure that our society or culture is quite ready for that sort of experimentation. Paradoxically enough, I suspect that "swinging" would be more acceptable to large numbers of the population than incomplete eroticism. I do not think it possible to write a book on sexuality at the present time without at least pointing out that this question is being asked. I am also convinced that it is impossible at the present to give any sort of decisive answer to it. In any case, people are experimenting. One will have to wait and see what results from the experiments. In my experience with the experimenters, many of them are immature and naive, engaging in dangerous self-deception. But there are others about whom I am certainly not ready to make such a quick judgment. On the contrary, I would tentatively observe that their relationships seem healthy, adult, and supportive of their fundamental and basic commitments. Only time will tell. (I have alluded to this "quiet Catholic question," as it has been called by another writer, in other books. Many people have written, partly out of curiosity, I suppose, but also because they are looking for support in their own situations, to ask whether I have had a direct experience myself with such a relationship. The truth of the matter is that I have not, and my writing on the subject is based on conversation and observation, not personal experience. I will confess to a certain lack of confidence in my own ability to cope with such a relationship, and I very much doubt whether I will ever experience one. The sorts of relationships in question are not for everyone—if, indeed for anybody. I am not ashamed to say that I doubt very much that they are possible for me.)

Sexuality, then, whether we be single or married, is a

powerful, demanding, barely controllable element in our lives. Wisdom consists not in repressing it, not in dealing with it crudely and casually but rather in understanding both its elemental force and the simultaneous necessity and frustration in restraining its vigor and drive. At the risk of gross oversimplification, I think one might state the following five rules for living with sexual hunger:

1. We must accept the tremendous power of our sexuality and acknowledge the weakness and inadequacy of our control over that power.

2. We must accept the fact that our sexuality flows in many strange eddies and currents and can be diverted down dark, hateful, and punitive streams.

3. We must accept the fact that the same ill-controlled and frequently deceptive power that we experience also exists in everyone else.

4. We must accept the fact that casual attitudes, simple formulae, easy answers, and magic techniques are inadequate responses to the fearsome power of sex.

5. We must accept the fact that whatever our sexual posture (married or celibate) hard work and constant effort at focusing energies is necessary for both healthy relationships with members of the other sex and for the diversion of our excess sexual energies into constructive and creative activities.

In a sense, of course, these rules are no rules at all. They are merely a restatement of the problem. But any attempt to deal with the problem of sexual hunger is bound to end up merely as a restatement of the problem. The essence of wisdom about sex is to understand that we are really in trouble when we think we have figured out the answers.

Our unruly sexuality may on many occasions be a burden to us. We might even be tempted to think that life would be much better if there was less passion in it; but, in truth, were we not sexual beings, life would be intolerably dull and inescapably lonely. Guilt over our "animality" is no response to the fact of human sexual hunger— though it certainly has a lengthy historical record for being a popular response. Guilt is an easy substitute for a much more difficult and complicated response—the recognition that our sexuality represents undifferentiated power, the goodness or badness of which depends to a considerable extent on our capacity to both acknowledge its importance and to humbly accept our inadequacies to do anything more than partially contain it.

It is possible to find in the Christian symbol system anything which will illumine the ambiguity of human sexual hunger? Mircea Eliade, in his book, *Mephistopheles and Androgyne* devotes a lengthy essay to the *coincidentia oppositorum*. He points out that the myth of the Androgyne is widespread in the world's religions as a symbol of man's desire to achieve unity by combining opposites. (Other symbols are the notion of the duality of God, a God of Good and a God of Evil, who in some religions are brothers). With his characteristic erudition, Eliade finds the androgyne, or similar symbols, in everything from Goethe's writing to the primitive beliefs of archaic tribes. He summarizes the finding of his chapter in the following paragraphs:

> What is revealed to us by all these myths and symbols, all these rites and mystical techniques, these legends and beliefs that imply more or less clearly the *coincidentia oppositorum*, the reunion of opposites, the totalization of fragments? First of all, man's deep dissatisfaction with his actual situation, with what is called the human condition. Man feels himself torn and separate. He often finds it difficult properly to explain to himself the nature of this separation, for sometimes he feels himself to be

cut off from "something" *powerful,* "something" utterly *other* than himself, and at other times from an indefinable, timeless "state," of which he has no precise memory, but which he does however remember in the depths of his being: a primordial state which he enjoyed before Time, before History. This separation has taken the form of a fissure, both in himself and in the World. It was the "fall," not necessarily in the Judaeo-Christian meaning of the term, but a fall nevertheless since it implies a fatal disaster for the human race and at the same time an ontological change in the structure of the World. From a certain point of view one may say that many beliefs implying the *coincidentia oppositorum* reveal a nostalgia for a lost Paradise, a nostalgia for a paradoxical state in which the contraries exist side by side without conflict and the multiplications form aspects of a mysterious Unity.

Ultimately, it is the wish to recover this lost unity that has caused man to think of the opposites as complementary aspects of a single reality. It is as a result of such existential experiences, caused by the need to transcend the opposites, that the first theological and philosophical speculations were elaborated. Before they became the main philosophical concepts, the One, the Unity, the Totality were desires revealed in myths and beliefs and expressed rites and mystical techniques. On the level of presystematic thought, the mystery of totality embodies man's endeavor to reach a perspective in which the contraries are abolished, the Spirit of Evil reveals itself as a stimulant of Good, and Demons appear as the night aspects of the Gods. The fact that these archaic themes and motifs still survive in folklore and continually arise in the worlds of dream and imagination proves that the mystery of totality forms an integral part of the human drama. It recurs under various aspects and at all levels of cultural life—in mystical philosophy and theology, in the mythologies and folklore of the world, in modern men's dreams and fantasies and in artistic creation.*

The yearning for sexual union, then, can be seen as but one manifestation of man's drive to break out of the limits his own individuation imposes on him and attempt to achieve a basic unity with the life forces of the universe. Men are impelled toward the woman in the elevator, or toward the luscious secretary, or women toward the man at the cocktail party, or the broad-shouldered male who sits next to her on the bus precisely because union with this other is a means of overcoming separation and putting the world back together again. This is not just poetry. It is a symbolic description of man's desire to break out of isolation and come into contact with Reality. A sexual partner, actual or potential, is both real and a manifestation of Reality. In a moment of ecstasy, we break out of our fragmented situation and become immersed in the primal life forces of the universe as a fused entity.

Most people don't think this way, of course, and it is perhaps just as well that they don't; but in the sexual union, men and women experience something that might be described on an intellectual level in those terms.

The Christian and Jewish symbol systems, as we noted in the previous chapter, take great delight in using sexual imagery to describe the relationship between God and his people. The very words used to describe the Sinai covenant myth emphasize the intimacy of the relationship: "I Yahweh am your God" (Ex. 20:3). They represent the central religious insight of Judaism and Christianity. They proclaim that there exists an "I-Thou" relationship between God and his people. Once that sentence has been spoken all else is commentary and explication. The result

* (From *Mephistopheles and the Androgyne: Studies in Religious Myth and Symbol* by Mircea Eliade, © in the English translation by Harvill Press, London, and Sheed & Ward, Inc., New York, 1965).

of this intimate relationship (and in the Old Testament world, covenants were the most intimate of human relationships), and also to some extent its cause, is a "hesed," a loving kindness between the closest of friends. Yahweh says that from his people he demands *ahabah*, "love"—but the very same word is used to describe the sexually aroused "love" of the bride and groom in the Song of Songs. Yahweh also proclaims himself *El Kana*, a phrase which we translate badly as "a jealous God" but could be better translated as "a passionate God."

But more than this has to be said. Although little attention has been paid to it, there is some evidence in the book of Genesis to support the notion that the writer of the book considered God to be androgynous. God is not to be thought of as "He," but rather as a "He-She." When a husband and wife, then, seek unity with one another, they are attempting to achieve in their union a perfection which exists permanently in God.

In light of this symbol, then, sexual hunger is not merely a hunger for the Absolute and the Real; it is also a hunger for union between the Male and the Female, which union exists permanently in God. In such a perspective, it becomes possible to say that when a husband and wife who are deeply in love with each other reach the climax of their sexual orgasm, they have achieved something that is, in the strict sense of the word, "godlike," because they have temporarily fused the Male and the Female. The *coincidentia oppositorum* has taken place, however briefly, in them, and the primal fracture has been temporarily fused.

Similarly, when our two friends in the elevator feel the brief but powerful electricity that flows from the radical possibility of sexual union between them, they are in fact experiencing a touch of the divine unity. It is not a trace of the divinity that should necessarily be pushed any further, but that they are capable of union with a member of the opposite sex reflects the unity of all things in God. It would seem to me that for the two people the proper reaction is neither to find a bedroom where they can have quick intercourse nor to be deeply chagrined at the power of their own passions; rather, I think, they should be grateful for the spark of the divine that is present in them and the revelation, however briefly, of the power of that spark.

The two of them have other things to do. To spend long hours dwelling on sexual fantasies, to enter a sexual relationship for which neither of them is ready would be inappropriate and foolish; but the brief and powerful experience of their own sexuality is not only not immoral or perverse but a revelation of fantastic (and unruly) forces within them, forces which quite literally can be called godlike.

And the only adequate response to such a brief revelation is gratitude that one has been born a man or born a woman.

A good deal more thought and theological reflection will have to take place before the notion of God as an androgyne will enable us to develop a comprehensive theory that we could call a "theology of sexual hunger." I do not propose to do anything more here than to point out that such a perspective might be far more helpful in trying to explain the meaning of our sexual hungers.

3

A Sexual Revolution?

Those who take their world view from the Sunday magazines, the national news journals such as *Time* and *Newsweek,* and the television talk shows know that there is a sexual revolution. Unencumbered by much in the way of empirical data, "experts" (and some with Ph.Ds) have announced that this is a New Age of Permissiveness made possible by the collapse of the "old morality" and the dissemination of the birth control pill. Our age, it would seem, is the first one to discover that sex can be fun, and we are all having a rip-roaring good time enjoying it. Most of the "experts" are in strong sympathy with the sexual revolution, though more recently, as the pandemic of venereal disease grips this country, some of them are beginning to have second thoughts.

There are a number of phenomena cited as evidence for the sexual revolution: There is the higher level of promiscuity among college students. Fewer women of the upper middle class are virgins when they marry. There is more "swinging" going on among suburban couples. Homosexuals and lesbians are more aggressive in resisting discrimination and proclaiming that, indeed, their sexual way is the better one. Pornography is more open than ever before and scarcely a serious motion picture can be made without considerable expanses of female anatomy displayed. There is, we are informed, much greater tolerance for sexual deviancy. Finally, some experts see in the communes and in women's liberation the first signs of "the end of the family."

Much of this "evidence" ought not to be taken too seriously. Research into the morality of college students indicates that if there was a change in their sexual behavior, it took place during the 1920s. The only thing that has changed today is their willingness to talk about it. Swingers, communards, and women's liberationists are a tiny minority of the population. The greater tolerance for pornography and deviancy may simply be the current upswing of the unending seesaw of strictness and laxity in man's attempt to impose morality by law. Pornography may be easier to come by now than in the past, but those for whom it was important could get it then if they wanted to. The shapely breasts of starlets in wide screen technicolor may say more about the difficulties Hollywood has encountered in competing with television than it does about the state of public morality. Nudity in movies merely makes the naked female body somewhat more accessible than it was in the old days of the burlesque houses. (And though the movies lack the third dimension of the burlesque stage, they probably do provide more attractive bodies to look at.)

The Sexual Revolution, then, as it is generally described is little more than a creation of the mass media, much like the Generation Gap, Future Shock, and the Radical Left Student. If one stops to think about it, it is amusing to believe that present day America is any more permissive than England of the Regency or the Restoration, Paris of the Bourbons, or Rome of the later Empire and the Borgias. Indeed, the information that has recently become available about the sexuality of nineteenth-century England suggests that the principal difference between us and our Victorian predecessors is that we may be more inclined to do openly what they did secretly—and which their predecessors also did openly with far more grace than we, perhaps.

There is, however, a real sexual revolution that the media have missed, in part because its complexity does not respond easily to media simplification. Fundamentally, the present sexual revolution results from an attempt to combine friendship with an explicit search for a high level of satisfaction for both sexes in marital genitality—a combination which has been reinforced and emphasized by the Freudian insights about the primal nature of the sexual drive. To put it briefly, the sexual revolution means now that we marry people who are our friends and attempt through mutual orgasm to deepen and enrich the friendship. Compared to this profound change in human behavior, the glimpse of an occasional bit of pubic hair in a Hollywood spectacular is of rather minor importance.

In tribal societies and in ancient cultures, friendship and genitality were rigidly separated. Women and men united to produce children and to maintain the family, but friendship was sought in groups with members of the same sex, in part because of the superstitious fear of something so powerful and demanding as heterosexual intimacy. In the Greek cities, the occasional homosexuality that existed in the friendship groups became commonplace. A man had two kinds of sex life: homosexual with his friends and heterosexual with his wife. The former was a pleasure, a joy, a means of authentic human behavior; the latter was an obligation to family and society. Those men who sought something more in heterosexual relationships turned to prostitutes with whom friendship was possible since such a relationship could be ended easily should it become dangerous.

In the early Christian era, there was a dramatic change in human attitudes. It was believed that in the power of the risen Lord men and women could gain control over their bodies and discipline and dominate their sexual appetites. Sex was no longer an impediment to human freedom because man could be the master of his sexuality. Since there was no longer "male" and "female" but "all one in Christ Jesus," friendship between sexes became possible. But it was friendship without sex. The "co-ed" monasteries and religious houses of the early church (and they were viewed with suspicion by such fiery types as St. Jerome) were attempts to achieve friendship and community across sexual lines by eliminating genitality and eroticism from the relationships between sexes.

Some of these agapite monasteries persisted in Ireland even into the sixth century, and those who belonged to them argued vigorously against suspicious critics that such joining of the sexes in the religious life was not only possible but virtuous. Hereafter follows the tale of the monk Scuthian (Scothin) and his demonstration of virtue to the skeptical Brendan (Brenainn). (The Irish writer George Moore, in his book, *The Storyteller's Holiday*, tells the same story in an uproariously funny contemporary Irish setting. Scuthian becomes a parish priest and Brendan becomes a chancery office official.) Vivian Mercier's *The Irish Comic Tradition* (Oxford: Oxford University Press, 1962, p. 43) gives us this episode:

> Now two maidens with pointed breasts used to lie with him (Scothin) every night, that the battle with the Devil might be the greater for him. And it was proposed to accuse him on that account. So Brenainn came to test him, and Scothin said: 'Let the cleric lie in my bed tonight,' saith he. So when he reached the hour of resting the girls came into the house wherein was Brenainn, with their lapfuls of glowing embers in their chasubles;

and the fire burnt them not, and they spill (the embers) in front of Brenainn, and go into the bed to him. 'What is this?' asks Brenainn. 'Thus it is that we do every night,' says the girls. They lie down with Brenainn, and nowise could he sleep with longing. 'That is imperfect, O cleric,' say the girls; 'he who is here every night feels nothing at all. Why goest thou not, O cleric, into the tub (of cold water) if it be easier for thee? 'Tis often that the cleric, even Scothin, visits it.' 'Well,' says Brenainn, 'it is wrong for us to make this test, for he is better than we are.' Thereafter they make their union and their covenant, and they part *feliciter*.

In the later Middle Ages there emerged in the Christian countries the idea of romantic love, the deep, intense, erotic friendship between a man and a woman without a genital relationship. The great courtly lovers of the Middle Ages were married, and apparently they made good enough husbands, wives, fathers and mothers; but their passionate friendships were not with spouses. The rules of the courtly love game forbade that these passionate romantic fantasies should ever end in intercourse. On the contrary, the whole game was spoiled if the lovers should ever sleep with one another. The most that would be permitted, and that only rarely, was fondling, brief nakedness, and a few moments lying next to each other in bed. According to the rules of the game, no more was wanted, expected, or tolerated.

From the modern point of view, both the agapite monasteries and courtly love were either impossible or unhealthy. But Herbert Richardson has argued persuasively that such a judgment may reflect more on us than on our predecessors. It may indicate that they understood far more about the complexities and possibilities of human sexuality than we do. In any event, according to Richardson, the idea of friendship without sexuality and eroticism without genitality were necessary preludes to the develop-

ment of the modern combination of friendship with geni
tality. As Richardson's title argues, *Nun, Witch, Playmate*,
the nun and the witch (the witch being the mirror image of
the courtly lover) had to emerge before a wife and a
husband could begin to think of each other as playmates.
The coeducational monastery and the romantic love of the
troubadors were necessary steps in the development of
the very modern and very recent idea that marriage, friendship, and the principle of genital satisfaction could all exist
in the same relationship.

That, then, is the real sexual revolution of our time.
Even in the nineteenth century there was a powerful conviction that marriage and friendship could be combined,
but in general, genital satisfaction in marriage was thought
to be either unimportant or only accidentally achieved. A
woman was thought not to be especially interested in
orgasm, and if a man wanted something besides the rather
limited genitality that marriage offered him, he was expected first to be thoroughly ashamed of himself and then to
guiltily seek satisfaction elsewhere. It is only in recent
times—to a great extent after the work of Freud became
well known—that we began to believe that it was possible
to combine marriage, friendship, and genital fulfillment.
Sex became a form of play and mutual orgasm was something that one was to seek principally from one's spouse,
who was now not only a friend but also a playmate.

This development is very recent and while many Americans are willing to endorse it in theory, the practice of
spouses as playmates may well be much less frequent.
Indeed, it seems a fair guess to assert that the majority of
American marriages are more likely to follow the Victorian
model than they are the playmate model. Husband and
wife are expected to be friends, but both of them are quite
reluctant to run the risk of being playmates.

It is obvious that a relationship that combines genitality,

playfulness, friendship, and the social obligations of marriage and parenthood is a complex and difficult relationship. Far more is expected of marriage than was ever expected in the past. In our day, it is assumed that marriage will combine the satisfactions that were distributed in several different relationships in years gone by. Men may continue, as they did in Paris of the nineteenth century, to have a wife for begetting children, a friend (usually male) for conversation, and a mistress for satisfactory orgasm; but while society may be tolerant of such a division of labor, the present ideal would still demand that the mistress and the friend and the wife be combined in the same person. Far from eliminating the family, the sexual revolution puts much more emphasis on the marriage union than it ever received in the past. One observer of contemporary sexual mores notes that the modern suburban matron routinely dons lingerie that not long ago only a whore would wear. This is not surprising, because the suburban matron, in addition to her duties as chauffeur, housekeeper, cook, social director, laundress, and mother, is also expected to provide a service for her husband not unlike that which a whore used to provide. Such an expectation introduces into her life a new and challenging and complicated role, one that the social ideal now demands of her, but for which she may very likely be psychologically and culturally unprepared. A whore's lingerie does not a skillful and competent mistress produce. Much less, however, does the recent ideal positing the man as playmate to his wife enable him to bring her the sexual satisfaction to which she now rightly aspires to have every bit as much right as he.

This sexual revolution may make life much more pleasurable, but it certainly makes it more complicated and demanding. The "new permissiveness" is usually casual sex—sex without obligation or responsibilities. In such a union, orgasm is quickly achieved, and the two partners go their ways to "seek new outlets." Such behavior is, for most people, not at all satisfying in the long run, but at least it is easy. It involves no expectations other than quick, uncomplicated fun. The "new permissiveness" in marriage, however, does not so much remove obligations and expectations as it imposes a whole new set of them. The suburban matron quickly learns that while the diaphanous nightgown may be part of her stock in trade, it scarcely makes her an effective mistress. And her husband also learns rather soon that simply knowing where to put his hands or his mouth is only the beginning of a sustained erotic relationship with his wife. The combination of sexual hunger and friendship in one relationship may well be an admirable ideal, it is certainly one that is relatively recent; but it is not an ideal easy to achieve or one that most married couples are ready to seriously seek.

There are a number of changes in attitudes—largely as a result of the insights of psychoanalysis—that do facilitate the combination of genitality and friendship. There is probably much more openness in the discussion of sex today than there has been in the recent past, though one is constantly astonished at how many husbands and wives seem incapable of saying anything to each other about their genital relationship. There is certainly more willingness to face explicitly the sexual components of our behavior. There is, I think, more awareness of the mutability of the social conventions by which society attempts to contain the primal sexual hungers of its members. There is certainly more concern about the sexuality of woman, perhaps more so than ever before, and it is possible that there is less fear of sexuality than in the past. All of these changes are a sign of progress, although one would be making a mistake to think that they are either as widespread or as profound as some popular discussion would indicate. There are, of course, some people who leap from the speculation of the mass media to practice. They do so generally with little thought and frequently with severe risk to themselves and their partners. But there are infinitely fewer suburban couples who engage in spouse-swapping than there are suburban couples who, despite the social emphasis on the new ideal of genitality and friendship and the ongoing public discussion of the "sexual revolution," still find themselves quite incapable of discussing even with each other what happens in bed at night. If the mass media's sexual revolution is not to be taken seriously, the real sexual revolution still has a long way to go before it becomes a pervasive cultural phenomenon. Routine practice tends to trail behind both theoretical ideals and mass-media popularization.

What stance does a modern American take in the face of the sexual revolution? He must first of all acknowledge that the ideal of combining genitality and friendship in marriage is a dominant ideal in his society and that it has a deep impact on both himself and his spouse no matter how far they may be from the ideal in practice. Young men and women approach marriage today with a powerful expectation that they will be able to be friends and playmates. To the extent that this expectation is not met, the marriage is bound to be frustrating no matter how much rationalization may be used to justify the rather low level of adjustment that they achieve.

A woman may have been unconsciously frustrated when she believed that she was not supposed to enjoy sex, but now that she knows she is supposed to enjoy it, the unconscious frustration in the absence of enjoyment becomes quite conscious and explicit, which of course makes the frustration worse. Similarly, a man had no particular reason to feel sexually incompetent if his wife did not have orgasms at a time when the mores ruled out the possibility of full genital satisfaction for a wife. But now that he knows that he is supposed to be a playmate for his wife, his failure to do so is bound to shake his confidence. Thus, there is no escaping the primary responsibility that American middle-class couples have to appraise their own marriage relationship in light of the ideal and ask whether they are moving in the direction of the ideal. There is no point in worrying about the other aspects of the sexual revolution until this primary responsibility is faced.

As for the other aspects of the sexual revolution, the wise man ought to suspend judgment, for as I see it, wisdom means that we neither write off the past nor remain incurably wedded to it. Nor do we take speculative theorizing by self-proclaimed "experts" to be scientific fact.

One of the principal problems of psychoanalysis as a scientific theory is that there is no way to disprove it. It is an inexorable law of scientific argumentation that if there is no way to disprove a theory then there is no way to prove it. If it is not possible to find evidence to refute a hypothesis then it is not possible to find evidence to confirm it. The psychoanalytic spokesman frequently bases his assertions on his own experience with patients, but there is no way one can replicate such experience, and hence no way one can prove or disprove the assertions of the therapist. Indeed, attempts to produce contrary evidence frequently result in the psychoanalytic "expert" asserting that such evidence may be true but collected from people burdened by guilt feelings caused by rigid moral codes created in the past. Or he asserts that the investigator with contrary evidence is himself the victim of his own unconscious drives. Such forms of ad hominem argument may well be effective, but they are not evidence in any sense that the word has in ordinary scientific discourse. The wise man will do well to keep in mind that unless an "expert" states his hypotheses in a way that can be empirically confirmed or refuted, he is offering merely personal opinion—informed, interesting, challenging it may be, but still personal opinion.

There are two implicit assumptions in much of the "expert" commentary on current sexuality. The first is the assumption of "evolutionary enlightenment." It presumes that man becomes wiser and more enlightened with each passing decade and century. Our predecessors were narrow, ignorant, rigid, and uninformed. We are open, enlightened, sophisticated, and informed. Therefore, whatever is occuring today represents not only an intellectual improvement over the past but a moral one too. Breaking away from the old moral tradition is in fact a sign of great human progress. Evolution toward greater enlightenment is not only good but inevitable. The direction of future evolution can be fairly well projected by looking at the young, who are, of course, the most recent manifestation of evolutionary progress. Thus, when relatively small segments of the college population "shack up" in relationships that may be relatively stable either as a prelude to marriage or as a substitute for it, these young people are eagerly interviewed by magazine writers and their words carefully jotted down as a sign of the most advanced human wisdom.

The second assumption is that of "scientism," which views man as essentially a highly developed animal. The scientism may not be quite so blatant as the serenely arrogant behaviorism of B. F. Skinner, but it assumes that human behavior can best be understood if man is compared with the other higher animals and his actions analyzed independent of the cultural and interpretive schemes that he has developed. Masters' and Johnson's research, for example even though it has unquestionably provided physiological information not previously available, assumes at its starting point that human sexuality can be observed and recorded in the same way one would observe and record the sexuality of any other animal. Researchers like Masters and Johnson would, of course, not deny the importance of the cultural, the social, and the interpersonal as a context for human genitality, but in fact they focus almost entirely on the physiological in their own research, arguing that the physical process of arousal and satisfaction is fundamentally the same between strangers and between spouses whether it occurs in the bedroom or the laboratory with motion picture cameras grinding away in the background.

Wisdom would suggest that both these assumptions ought to be questioned. The wise man is neither an undertaker who wishes to bury completely the traditions of the past nor a miracle worker who wishes to revive them completely; he is rather, as Paul Ricoeur says of the interpreter of religious symbols, a man who is both willing to suspect the past and willing to listen to it. Father John Shea in his book, *What a Modern Catholic Believes about Heaven and Hell*, describes a Christian response to changing cultural values which seems especially appropriate to apply to the alleged sexual revolution:

There is a strong conserving strain in the Catholic tradition. The Christian is an incurable saver. He drags his whole past with him into the future. He would move quicker if he scrapped many of the things he carried, but he cannot bear to lose an alternative perspective or a possible truth. An ancient religious practice or a dusty doctrine may capture and communicate an undying aspect of the human situation. At the present moment its meaning may be obscure but that does not mean its truth is dead. The Christian hordes wisdom; he is reluctant to part with anything.

The wise man then, Christian or not, is both suspicious of the past and willing to listen to it. He is also suspicious of the present and willing to listen to it. He does not easily give up past traditions, but he is ready to reinterpret them and to refine them when the available evidence seems to indicate that it is time for reinterpretation and refinement. Such an attitude is hard to maintain if like Alvin Toffler you believe we are caught in future shock and if like Margaret Mead you believe that now we have a culture oriented totally toward the future. Under such circumstances one wishes to jettison the past completely. The position taken by Shea and Paul Ricoeur implies the fundamental unity of human experience and insists that the wise man learns from both the past and the present. Ultimately one must choose either one perspective or the other, and in making the choice one might keep in mind the fact that future believers in the inevitability of evolution toward enlightenment will just as surely and just as categorically reject Mead, Toffler, and all the other "experts" of today as these worthies reject the conventional wisdom of our day. Today's progressive insights become tomorrow's traditional wisdom in the evolutionary perspective. If we expect the future to listen to and respect us, we should listen to and respect our predecessors.

Furthermore, while it may be quite possible to study the sheer physiology of sexual union in the laboratory with only slight attention paid to the interpersonal and cultural context in which the union occurs, the conversion of these laboratory findings into a program for human behavior is not likely to be helpful and may even be counterproductive unless other factors are taken into account. Masters and Johnson make the leap from laboratory to program without bothering to pay much attention to the social, the cultural, the interpersonal, and the value systems in which their "subjects" live. (And their predecessor Dr. Kinsey did this to a much greater extent.)

Scientism and behaviorism find it very difficult to face the fact that man is not just an animal. Alone among all the animals he has the capacity for language, for investing his behavior with meaning and value, for establishing relationships to which his language and the symbol systems it creates give meaning and interpretation that go far beyond mere physical contact. Man's capacity for language and his power of interpretation affect him in two critical ways. It first of all endows him with a capacity for fantasy, which other animals lack, and, secondly, it gives him the possibility, while imposing upon him the necessity, of interpreting his behavior, of assigning it meaning. The refusal of some of the extreme devotees of scientistic philosophy to assign any meaning or value to human genitality is in itself an interpretation. The isolation of the physiological from the other components in human relationships in the Masters and Johnson laboratory is a value decision and interpretation of utmost importance.

It is perhaps understandable that science is fighting the rigid morality of the past, because that rigid morality often stood in the way of the proper development of scientific enterprise. It is also perhaps understandable that science prescind from man as a language-creating, meaning-endowing animal, because his capacity to develop symbols to explain and interpret his behavior for himself and others is extremely complicated and difficult to understand. It is, after all, relatively easy to persuade couples to copulate in the laboratory; in fact, apparently, such an experience can be extremely satisfying on a short-term basis (fantasies about copulating with an attractive stranger in full public view are evidently not rare in the human imagination), but it would be much more difficult to study the complex interactions of friendship and genitality as it takes place in an ongoing relationship where two people are trying to overcome their fears and timidities and grow in trust and pleasure with one another. Of course, until such research is attempted—if it can be done ethically—we only have a limited knowledge of the workings of human genitality. Behaviorists can argue better from a limited knowledge of the sheer physiology of copulation than no knowledge at all. The point is understandable, but the wise man knows that while all things the laboratory researcher says may be true, it still doesn't come close to saying the whole truth.

There is ambiguity and difficulty in standing between the past and the present, being suspicious of the cheap generalizations of both and still listening intently to the insights of both. It is especially difficult to do this when one accepts the serious challenge of trying simultaneously to be a spouse and a playmate, a mistress and a friend. In it most rigid form, the past wisdom says, "All will be well in your marriage if you are faithful to one another." In its most rigid form, some of the modern conventional wisdom says, "If you trade spouses occasionally or sleep around before you marry, or if you become reasonably adept at fellatio, then your genital life will be exciting and satisfying." But neither the simplicism of the mass media nor the simplicism of a narrow behaviorist approach to human activity will deal adequately with the complexity of human sexuality.

The legalism of the past and the simplicism of the present have one important thing in common. They both assume that the problems of sexuality can be solved in terms of who you sleep with and what particular organs are combined in what ways. As anyone who has pondered his own sexual experience seriously knows, it is not all that easy—and it never will be so long as man has both a fantasy life and the power to interpret and give meaning to his behavior.

4

How to Be Sexy

Being "sexy" is no problem for animals. Most of the time the animal is not particularly interested. When the female is in heat, the male is aroused and their instinctual systems make it quite clear to them how they ought to behave. When the period of arousal is past, "sexy" behavior becomes irrelevant and the instinctual system no longer guides them toward sexual activity.

Mankind is quite different. His sexual instincts are powerful but not programmed for automatic sexiness. His fantasy life gives him some broad guidelines as to how to act, but his capacity for interpretation and for definition can impede him and may even suggest that sexiness is somehow or other "dirty."

Mankind, then, has a number of serious problems in coping with his own eroticism:

1. His sex drive can be aroused at any time. As a result, he has far more sexual energy available to him than do other animals, and he must learn to exercise restraint on his sexual behavior, a restraint which we call "social convention."

2. Mankind's sexuality is set in a matrix of his behavior as a symbol-creating, meaning-giving animal. How he behaves sexually depends to a con-

siderable extent on how he defines his own sexuality. He is not automatically "sexy"; he can only become sexy or let it emerge in a context of meaning and interpretation.

3. Because of his power to create symbols and the permanency of his sexual hunger, mankind has an extraordinarily active, vigorous, and creative fantasy life. Animals do not create poetry, and because they do not they are free from mankind's burden of seeing sexuality everywhere and his profound need for a variety and playfulness in his sexual relationships.

There is little variety in animal sexuality. Some species do have a certain ritual of playfulness that precedes copulation, though it is a ritual that is fundamentally physiological in its purpose and is required to give both animals time to become fully aroused. In the human species, physiological arousal comes rather quickly once the appropriate stimuli are produced. Playfulness in the human sexual relationship, then, is only indirectly physiological in its function and is the result of man's limitless capacity for fantasy, for symbol, and for variety.

If mankind did not have this capacity for variety and playfulness and the need to exercise this capacity, human genitality would be a relatively simple affair. It is evidence of the power of his fantasy life and his capacity to create symbols that something as physiologically powerful as his sex drive can become dull and even monotonous in the absence of variety and playfulness. The attempt to move playfulness out of the whorehouse and into the home and to create variety even in the suburban bedroom is evidence that monotony and boredom is no longer tolerable in marriage. But the challenge that the sexual revolution imposes on huband and wife is a severe one. A routine genital relationship is easy to sustain; one fulfills one's obligations, one gets a certain amount of satisfaction, one does not have to spend time, energy, and imagination maintaining variety and playfulness in the ambiance of one's marriage. One can have sex without having to be sexy.

To be sexy is to create an erotic atmosphere around oneself, to radiate an atmosphere of sexual attractiveness, to invite potential sexual partners, to enjoy playfulness and variety in a genital relationship. The sexy person says in effect, "I am not merely a woman or a man. I am a playmate, a lover with whom you can have all kinds of fun. With me, even some of your wildest fantasies can be enjoyed in reality. I am not just an outlet like everyone else of my sex. I am a challenge and an opportunity."

A second factor, and perhaps a more important one, in becoming sexy is our early childhood experiences. We absorb attitudes toward our bodies and our sex from our parents about the same time that we absorb our language and our fundamental religious beliefs. If our parents are at ease and at peace with their bodies, then we absorb the same attitudes. We are aware of our body's dimensions, its proportions, and its energies. We are confident in its strength and delighted with its potentiality for playfulness and pleasure. We will not be afraid of our bodies, not very ashamed of them, and capable of using them as tools of communication with our fellow men.

Finally, we become sexy by acquiring the skills of sexiness. For most, this is a painful and difficult experience. It is not so hard to learn how to act sexy. The Don Juan, the tease, the actor, the model—all are required by their neurosis or their occupation (and quite possibly both) to go through the motions of being sexy. But both the Don Juan and the tease really have no confidence in their bodies and must temporarily build it up by exploiting others. The actor and the model may indeed be radiating an eroticism which they feel in their bones and muscles and to which their intellects and their personalities are committed; but they may also be simply playing a game. Pretending to be sexy is infinitely easier than being sexy. The starlet who so calmly and blatantly displays her charms before the camera may indeed have confidence in her own sexuality and may be eager to enter a love relationship in which she can combine intensity and playfulness—and commitment. But then again she may not, and the body that we see so confidently displayed on the screen may very well contain a personality that is frightened, filled with shame, distrust, and suspicion—capable only rarely of escaping from frigidity. Sexiness is the capacity to communicate our deepest feelings of eroticism to others in a nonthreatening and attractive way. Our capacity for fakery is such that we can seem to communicate with our bodies when in fact we are using them as barriers to keep others away.

To be sexy, then, is to be aware of one's body as an instrument of playfulness and delight, to be able to communicate this awareness to others, and then to commit oneself to a gift of that body in a mutual search for pleasure, delight, variety, and playfulness. Some are fortunate in that either their genetic equipment or their early childhood experience bring them to adult genitality well-equiped to be sexy, but most must learn how; and to learn how to overcome shame and fear, disgust and uncertainties is a slow and difficult process, which cannot be shortcutted by intense weekends of feeling and pawing. Shame is not a demon to be exorcized easily.

Shame is basically a feeling of inadequacy. One is afraid to reveal one's sexual organs because they may not be good enough. Physical shame is intimately connected with human shame; fear to reveal sexual organs results from feelings of human inadequacy. Some feeling of personal and physical inadequacy is probably part of the human condition. Man becomes conscious of himself by individuating himself over against others, and in that act of "alienation," he acquires fears that in his attempts to accomplish union now as an individuated person, he may not have all that it takes. In addition to this "existential" shame, which is part of the human condition, there can be a considerable amount of "psychic" shame. Some cultures and societies greatly reinforce the existential shame by placing strong emphasis on the evil of the human body and the risks of human sexuality. Within these societies certain kinds of early childhood experience produce intense feelings of guilt and inadequacy. Thus, in contemporary America, despite our happy talk of "permissiveness," many (indeed, most) people approach the physical and psychological stripping that marital intimacy demands with a combination of fear and disgust. Some people manage to overcome these reactions, but others are plagued with them and often use them as means of self-defense for all of their lives. Most of us are not very good at coping either with our own shame or that of our potential partners. This paralyzing shame coexists with an intense desire in our fantasy lives for self-revelation—both psychically and physically. Even if we are able to repress the fantasy of being stripped from our daytime imaginings, we certainly cannot eliminate it from our dreams, and we must admit that while it is a terrifying dream, it is also a delightful one. In the struggle between shame and self-revelation in our fantasy world, self-revelation wins, but in the real world shame is all too frequently the victor.

To complicate matters, there coexists with shame another and fundamentally healthy instinct toward, what I shall call for lack of a better word, "privacy." In most human societies, even those where there is relatively little shame and also relatively few arguments, men and women are concerned about surrounding their most intimate activities with some kind of privacy. This search for privacy, which in many societies is quite unaffected by physical conditions and customs that from our point of view would destroy privacy, may be in part a recognition of the intense power of man's sexual hunger. It also may be a result of the realization that a person's sex is deeply linked to his integrity and his individuality as a human being. The covering of sexual organs would then be merely an assertion of personal dignity and independence.

Privacy, as I have defined it here, and shame need not be connected. They represent two opposing thrusts, one emphasizing human dignity and the other human ugliness; but unfortunately for us the two emotions are tangled together and confused. Privacy is no obstacle to appropriate self-revelation. Indeed, when circumstances arise in which self-revelation becomes desirable, then privacy vanishes; but the motivations which prescribe privacy can be twisted and are twisted by most of us to reinforce shame. A young woman—unless she has that sickness called exhibitionism—is quite properly reluctant to reveal her sex organs to a man with whom she has no desire to share intimacy. She is not ashamed of her sexuality but she does not propose to reveal herself to everyone—a perfectly healthy attitude. But she is plagued by a confusion of privacy and shame. Part of the reason she carefully draws the shade in her room at night is that by so doing she maintains her own dignity and integrity. Simultaneously, she fears the thought of someone's glimpsing her body. To make sure this does not happen, she dresses with all possible speed in the bathroom, perhaps, or even under the covers. It will be hard for such a young woman to adjust to the total change that marriage will work in her life. For with marriage all the reasons for privacy (at least in the narrow sense in which it has been defined here) will be eliminated, yet her shame will persist, and even though she may realize it shouldn't—shame is a powerful emotion that will not be eliminated easily. Shame, rooted in our existential self-disgust, reinforced by our culture and our up-bringing, remains a powerful barrier to both physical and psychological self-revelation.

For men in our culture the problem is a bit different. They are somewhat less concerned than women about their bodies being seen by other men (though not completely unconcerned about it either). They are also probably somewhat less disturbed by the physical nakedness that is expected in marriage. However, there is no reason at all to think that there is any less psychic and human shame in men than in women. Indeed, if anything, it may be an even more difficult problem because the active aggressive model provided by our culture for the adult male may make it harder for him to reveal himself than it is for his wife. He may be able to bluff his way through the problem of physical openness a little better than she, but the stone wall of shame is as much a barrier to psychic and human openness for a man as it is for a woman. Perhaps the beginning of growth in love for a couple is the acknowledgment by the man that he is as much troubled by shame as is his woman.

Shame, then, is the enemy of sexiness—shame over our bodies and shame over ourselves. Because of shame some try to get through genital obligations as quickly and as routinely and as seriously as possible. When one is ashamed of oneself and ashamed of what one is doing—no matter how much he or she may be enjoying it—there is little inclination to seek either variety or playfulness; hence, very controlled and restrained attempts to create an atmosphere of eroticism and no wish to communicate the intensity of sexual hunger or the vividness of fantasies, because this would be a form of openness and self-revelation that would obviously repel and disgust others. A man is therefore content to play the role of rough, tough, direct male. A woman is content with being the teasing flirt. Both roles may occasionally look sexy, but in fact there is rather little real eroticism in either of them. A man who does not communicate a capacity for tenderness and sensitivity really isn't very sexy, and a woman who cannot go beyond teasing to clear, direct, and vigorous passion appears erotic only to the most shallow and superficial of potential partners.

Sexiness, then, is a communication of one's nature as a bodily sexed creature. It is erotic self-display. Given the intensity of hunger for sexual satisfaction and the poignancy of desire for love, it is sometimes difficult for most not to engage in erotic self-display. In other words, human beings are sexy creatures, but they can use their capacity for language and meaning to repress this sexiness, to hide it, to cover it, to pretend that it isn't there. Of course, a heavy price must be paid for this pretense; but for many, such a price is preferable to running the risk of ridicule and rejection involved in erotic self-display. It is also easier to solve the problem by denying it rather than by facing the complicated question of when self-display is elegant, tasteful, and effective and when it is repellent, inept, and counterproductive. Both the nudists and the prudes have simple answers to the question, but, as in so many other areas, simplicity is achieved by denying the complexity of the human condition.

One of the most obvious forms of erotic self-display is clothes. In our time, despite the herculean efforts of *Esquire* and, later, *Playboy*, only relatively slight progress has been made toward converting men's fashions into effective means for erotic display. Dramatically colored sports garb and the present, apparently waning fashion of bright shirts are evidence that men are not unaware that color and variety enhance their sexual attractiveness, but most of the time men do their best to appear as dull, colorless, and unsexy as possible in their daily garb.

For women the matter is quite different. Our society permits them to be much more concerned about varieties of self-display in the clothes they wear. Yet despite the frequently blatant sexual allusions in the garment industry's advertising, much of a woman's concern about clothes is that they be quite devoid of erotic content. Women frequently dress to impress other women with their choice of clothes much more than they do to impress men with their sexual desirability. Thus, clothes, so clearly and obviously a means for communicating both variety and playfulness, are frequently devoid of any explicit erotic intent or content.

The importance of clothes to a woman's own sexual self-image ought not to be underestimated. To put attractive garments on the most intimate parts of one's body is, or at least can be, an act of confidence in the fundamentally attractive and nonshameful nature of these organs. Not only are the clothes attractive; she, as a sexed person, is attractive. Her body is nothing to be ashamed of, but rather something to take delight in. However hasty her glance, she cannot escape the fantasy that what she sees so seductively arrayed in the mirror will be irresistible to a man.

Perhaps it would be a good thing if the woman spent a little more time admiring what she sees in the mirror. The problem for most of us, after all, is rather too much shame instead of too much narcissism. But the image she sees in the mirror is indeed admirable—one of the most attractive sights in physical creation—a sight whose attractiveness she has ingeniously enhanced by her choice of garb. She should admire what she sees. It is very much to be feared that if she is not capable of being struck forcefully by her own attractiveness, she will not be likely to allow others to delight in the scene.

But it is to be feared that many women resolutely ignore the possibilities. I remember one disgruntled husband complaining to me some time ago that, for all the elaborateness of her outer garments, his wife's bras and girdles (this was a time when both those garments were considered more mandatory than at present) were tattered and dull. She wore nothing but lusterless and unimaginative white. Her girdles were frazzled and frequently had holes in them, and her bras were held together by safety pins. "She cares a lot about what she looks like to others," he complained, "but she doesn't give a damn about what she looks like to me." It was a blunt complaint and perhaps one that many men would be afraid to speak. The marriage relationship was a troubled one, and the woman's lack of concern about the garments that only she or her husband would see merely indicated the trouble. But she was neither so naive nor so unimaginative as to have any doubt about the message she was sending, and he received it. An aspect of the relationship that could have enhanced its variety and playfulness was in fact doing just the opposite and making it even more routine and dull.

Does it matter to a man what the color of a few ounces of tricot and spandex found beneath his wife's dress is? What difference does it make whether all her bras and panties are white or a mixture of mint, peach, apricot, poppy, coral, etc.? If the only thing that counts in a genital relationship is the coupling of organs, then it doesn't matter; but if variety, playfulness, challenge, stimulation are important aspects of a genital relationship, then the frail garments that stand between a man and the body of his woman are potentially of considerable importance. A woman's use of lingerie to attract, stimulate, and seduce her husband is only an indicator of something much more fundamental and basic in their relationship. If she is not making use of the opportunities the ingeniously designed underwear provides for her, then she should certainly ask herself whether the wasted opportunity is a sign of a much more fundamental problem.

And so, for that matter, should her husband. Our increased knowledge of the sexuality of woman (to be discussed in a later chapter) would suggest that the last garments that stand between a wife's and her husband's body can take on powerful sexual overtones for her as well. The variety of her husband's underclothes can have considerable erotic impact on her. In any event, men's clothing manufacturers have recently introduced a variety of color and design into men's underwear that make them obvious garments for erotic display. Multihued tricot briefs are no longer to be found exclusively in the women's section of a department store or in the woman's part of the bedroom dresser. If such colorful masculine underwear continues to be marketed it means that men are buying it in considerable quantity. Thus a catalogue from one very respectable men's clothing firm depicts "ultra print," "rainbow stripe," "criss-cross," and "see-through mesh" bikini's for men as well as a collection of nylon "kaftans," which are described as making those who wear them "sexy" and "irresistible." One is tempted to see a suggestion of homosexuality in some of this, except that the unclad (though modestly protected) women who gaze longingly at the models garbed in the "kaftans in the same catalogue obviously have something else in mind. Clothes do not the lover make (male or female), and advertising which appeals to the fantasy life may be aimed only at fantasies never realized; but the catalogue indicates beyond all doubt that there is now market value in appealing to the male need for erotic self-display—even if the erotic self is not displayed in very effective fashion to anyone but the self.

It is interesting to speculate that the apparent increase in concern about the erotic attractiveness of the male body may be a result of the increase in demands from women for sexual satisfaction and the inevitable threat to the masculinity of many men that such demands involve. Alas for the complexity of the human condition, a royal blue nylon toga or a rainbow strip "super bikini" may make a man marginally more attractive to his woman, but it will not make him fundamentally "sexy" or "irresistible" if he has not already come to terms with both his sexuality and hers. Erotic self-display that hides fear, defensiveness, and uncertainty is a poor substitute for real eroticism. However, that men are more aware of the importance of self-display (should one say, "once again"?) is a sign of some progress.

In a good erotic relationship, the two people involved do all they can to make the environment of their relationship conducive to maintaining a high level of eroticism. Intimate apparel, whether a man's or a woman's, can obviously play a reasonably important part in the self-display that creates such an environment. Living with one's sexuality requires both that one recognize the availability of such resources and then uses them. But of course the critical question is how to use them. A suburban matron may wear lingerie that years ago only a whore would wear and her husband may affect garments that only a gigolo would manifest, but it doesn't follow that either partner may be willing to risk a relationship that psychically and physically will take advantage of the erotic potential. The sheer bra and shocking red shorts do not represent much of an improvement over the past if husband and wife are willing to indulge in some forms of erotic self-display in only very restricted and constrained fashion.

From the question of partial undress to that of total undress is only one step logically and psychologically. Nudity is a question of perennial interest and one the complete investigation of which would require a book in itself. Both the nudes and the prudes take extreme positions. The nude sees no problem at all in nakedness, and in his camps solves the problem by denying its existence. The prude, for his part, thinks that under virtually every circumstance a display of the human body is dangerous and evil. The nude sings the praises of naturalness, the prude dashes around with a measuring tape.

Both understand rather little about the paradoxes of nature and of human sexuality—a longing to undress and to appear to others either partially or totally bare, but on the other hand a terrible fear of exposure. (And of course there is a psychological parallel in the revelation of our personhood, in which the paradox of the desire for openness and the desire to hide is even more powerful.) Both opposing urges are strong, both are socially functional, and both correspond to deep personality needs. The solution to the conflict between the two lies not in abolishing one or the other but in determining—with the assistance of social conventions—that under some circumstances it is perfectly appropriate to undress in the presence of others while in other circumstances it is not appropriate at all. The precise nature of the conventions which regulate veiling and unveiling may change and may at given times be either unduly rigid or unduly lax, but the point is that the conventions themselves make it possible to reach agreement on how to combine these two urges.

The bathing beach in modern Western society is a classic example of the functionally legitimated opportunity for dressing and undressing in public. Most people are perfectly willing to display themselves in extremely erotic attire on the beach while they would not dream of wearing the same clothes to a store only several blocks away. It is not merely that they enjoy exposing most of their bodies to the sun, sea, and sand, though obviously that is part of the reason. The beach is a place where bodies may be seen. A moderately prudish woman who would be very embarrassed if the top button of her dress came open would not hesitate to strip off a terrycloth robe on the beach to reveal a very brief swimsuit. The ensuing delight on the part of those males around her will seemingly not permeate her consciousness. For a brief moment she is engaged in a strip tease and she likes it. So do they.

In some societies, conventions are far too rigid and in others they are far too lax. A good deal more relatively harmless erotic self-display on the beach today is far superior to the lack of it there fifty years ago, but whether erotic display on the beach is an indication of how much genital satisfaction is available in a society is certainly open to question. What kind of woman will the girl in the bright bikini be when she is in her husband's arms at night? The young matron who so casually discards her terrycloth robe may find it hard to disrobe with equal casualness in the presence of only her husband. In her stripping at the beach she is in a situation which is not particularly threatening; she can display herself without running much risk to the core of her selfhood. If her eroticism can be as casual in the bedroom with her husband as it is on the beach, then she really isn't pretending. If there are a considerable number of women in the society who can live up to their erotic displays on the beach in their relationships with their husbands, then a pretty convincing case could be made that such eroticism is healthy for the society. But there is some reason to doubt that at the present time such an argument would be valid.

We must face the fact that the nature of prudery in our society is such that for too many married couples inhibitions are so strong that there is probably much less nakedness in their relationship than would be healthy. Despite the powerful and delightful dreams and fantasies, physical self-revelation and self-disclosure is done hastily and almost surreptitiously. Dressing and undressing, activities potentially suffused with eroticism, are about as erotic in experience as eating breakfast. In fact, the variety of dress, semidress, and undress that could occur between lovers is limited only by the creativity of their fantasy lives and time. In practice, for many people whatever nakedness there is takes place only in the bedroom, only fleetingly, and only in semidarkness.

The opposite extreme may be less frequent, but it is equally an escape from wonder and mystery. Casual nudity around the house and in the presence of children is taken by some people to be a sign of progressive and liberal attitudes. It is in fact evidence of the absence of taste and sensibility and perhaps also a subtle seductiveness toward children. People who engage in such behavior make the journey from prudery to exhibitionism without pausing for a moment to consider the possibility of elegance and grace.

But what about nudity beyond the relationship between husband and wife? What about groups of married couples looking for erotic excitement short of swinging in, perhaps, sheltered backyard swimming pools or on deserted sections of beach late at night. What about young people trying to satisfy their curiosity about the opposite sex? What about friends who are not married to each other and do not contemplate marriage, but who feel that partial nakedness or even total nakedness is a form of communication of affection? One must first of all observe that such behavior is not especially new or revolutionary. It has gone on in the past, goes on today, and is likely to go on always. Unlike the nudists or certain kinds of encounter marathons, the "experimenters" described above do not reject social convention; they simply set aside such conventions temporarily and in some privacy. They do so on the grounds that the intimacy of the particular relationship is such that the convention really doesn't apply. As a matter of fact, there is perhaps as much fun in the excitement of violating a convention, in liberating oneself temporarily from official constraints as there is in the explicitly erotic aspect of such experiences. Nude swimming by moonlight, we are told, can be a hell of a lot of fun. Perhaps it is; indeed, it would be strange if it were not, but there is good reason to believe that such forms of temporary unconventional behavior rapidly lose their payoff in thrill and excitement. It is to be supposed that one must follow one's own taste and sensitivities in such matters. Surely such experiences of nakedness that are not part of a genital relationship are no cure for anything. Nobody's emotional problems are going to be resolved by these experiments. On the contrary, if this kind of behavior is to be both harmless and healthy, it will be so only when fundamental sexual adjustments of the people involved are relatively good—but then perhaps there would be less reason for experimentation. In the present cultural circumstances, nakedness apart from a permanent or quasi-permanent genital relationship would probably not be most people's cup of tea however actively they may fantasize about it. The real problem is not what might happen on the beach in the moonlight but what happens between husband and wife in the privacy of their home. If the young man and woman swim in the nude before they are married, I don't think I would be terribly troubled by their behavior—if I were confident that five years after they were married their psychological relationship would be such that they were as interested then in erotic self-display as they were on the moonlit beach. Variety and playfulness between married lovers exist in the area between psychological openness and trust on the one hand and intercourse on the other. When playfulness declines, the other aspects of the relationship may be in serious trouble.

In order to be sexy, to create an ambiance of eroticism around one's person, it is necessary to accept the body as good, sexuality as good, our own personhood as good, and then to understand that whether one likes it or not one is constantly emitting sexual messages. The erotic message may be one of openness, playfulness, and trust or it may be one of fear, suspicion, and shame; it may be a message of disgust and revulsion or, finally, a message of weariness and boredom. But there will be a message, and what it is depends on what is chosen, even though some refuse to face the fact that they have chosen.

In the final analysis, the question is the capacity to arouse wonder and create surprise. Weariness, distractions, problems, home, office, family, school—all these things bring strong pressure to settle down to a routine, the ordinary, a life out of which all excitement, all wonder, all surprise, has been taken. The sexy person is still capable of surprising others and also himself. In all his relationships there is wonder, both physical and psychological, because one cannot ever be sure of exactly what will happen. Predictability destroys wonder, surprise, variety, and playfulness.

Let us imagine two lovers. They know at the beginning of the day that it is very likely they will make love tonight. Is the routine absolutely predictable, or at the deep end of consciousness are there a number of questions that delight, amuse, and puzzle them in the course of the day? The husband, for example, may be asking, how will she respond? Will she be hungry and passionate, perhaps even more aggressive than I? Will she be shy and passive? Will she want me to take her directly and forcefully—perhaps even on the living room floor after the children are asleep, or shall I make it a long and involved seduction scene? Will I wait until we get into bed, or will I begin to undress her? What will she look like? What will she be wearing? Will she have on that transparent lingerie in which she looks so delicious? Will she let me take off her bra?

And the woman will be semiconsciously dwelling on similar questions. When will he start? Will it begin even before supper or will he wait? Where will his hands and his mouth go first? Will he be in one of those moods when he wants to strip me leisurely? Shall I turn the tables on him tonight and strip him first, or will I surprise him with my plan to trap him at his work in the library when I approach him wearing only panties and a martini pitcher—or maybe only the martini pitcher? Will I kneel on top of him, forcing my body down on his?

What is important is not the content of the questions, for that will vary from couple to couple and from time to time. The critical point is that questions like these are still worth asking. If everything that will happen is absolutely predictable and routine, the wonder and the surprise will have gone out of the relationship.

It is also necessary that the questions be asked with a lightness and wit. If the erotic self-display that goes on between genital lovers is heavy, somber, serious (as it always sounds in the sex manuals), it will also be dull and uninteresting. Playfulness that isn't playful is probably worse than no play at all. Lovers play with each other because it is fun, not because they are applying a lesson they learned in school or proving their masculinity or femininity or doing something that is expected of people of their education and sophistication. The nerves and muscles of the human body, and particularly of the human sex organs, were made to be played with by a member of the opposite sex. While there is obviously no obligation for anyone to engage in such play, it seems utterly foolish for those who are genital lovers not to take the opportunity that is offered them. Yet it is to be feared that prudery, fear, ignorance, and distrust make married love for most people much less playful than it ought to be.

But the fundamental question may not be so much one of sex as it is one of belief. A dull, monotonous, predictable genitality makes sense in a dull, monotonous, predictable universe. If man is caught either by the fates or by chance, if life is without purpose or design, it is a closed

and cool universe, indeed, and there is nothing to be surprised about and no possibility of surprise; and since there
is nothing wonderful going on, there is nothing to wonder
about either. Why bother trying to keep wonder and surprise alive amid all the distractions and diversions in one's
sexual life when the world is in fact a dull, drab, unsur-
prising place?

There is, of course, an answer to this out of the Christian
symbol system. Father John Shea in his book *What a Modern Catholic Believes about Heaven and Hell* concludes by
suggesting that we should all approach death with a well-
developed capacity for surprise. I think one could push
Father Shea's point a bit further and suggest that the essence of the Christian life is developing a capacity for surprise. We really have no choice if we wish to be Christians,
because God's intervention in our lives was a total and
complete surprise. Yahweh on Sinai caught Israel flat-
footed, and the resurrection of Jesus caught the apostles
equally flat-footed. Yahweh proclaimed on Sinai and Jesus
renewed the proclamation that life is wonderful and filled
with surprises, the greatest of which is God's incredible
love for us. The Christian can only respond to the surprise
of God's intervention by keeping alive his faith in the possibility of surprise and developing his capacity for bringing
delightful surprises to others.

It is no poetic exaggeration, then, but strict theological
truth to say that the capacity to cause surprise and delight
in others by erotic self-display is a continuation of Yahweh's work. It is not merely that by creating wonder in
others our faith is manifested in the basic wonderfulness
of the universe—the great surprise that Yahweh began on
Sinai is continued and expanded.

It is no exaggeration either, then, to say that the wife
clad in panties and martini pitcher is imitating Yahweh's
behavior. Indeed, if she only has the martini pitcher, she is

imitating him even more appropriately, because then both her surprise and her gift are total, just as Yahweh's gift and surprise to us were total.

It will be argued that it would never occur to most women that such revelation of themselves is a model of Yahweh's self-revelation to Israel. It will also be argued that precious few wives will ever work up the courage to create such a surprise.

Both arguments are undoubtedly true, but that is hardly Yahweh's fault.

5

The Insatiable Female?

In the previous chapter I suggested that part of the real sexual revolution is the legitimation of sexual pleasure for women and an increase of concern about the social and cultural forces which impede the development in many women of a satisfying genitality. It is worthwhile to summarize some of the research findings that have recently become available. Many people may have reservations about the way the data were obtained, but there seems little reason to doubt their accuracy.

1. It is apparently true that it takes somewhat longer for a woman to arrive at a full state of physiological sexual arousal than a man, but not much longer.

2. Sexual arousal in a woman declines much more rapidly than in the man when the source of stimulation is removed.

3. But in the presence of proper stimulation, a woman can remain aroused and experience orgasmic satisfaction indefinitely. A healthy woman is physiologically capable of at least two or three orgasms while her husband has one, and under some circumstances she may experience as many as six.

4. The physiology of a woman's genital organism is such that she can

103

experience orgasms indefinitely, with the only limit being physical exhaustion. Researchers report that some women can "enjoy" as many as fifty orgasms in an hour.

5. It is therefore literally true to say that a woman is sexually insatiable. She may be psychologically satisfied with one orgasm but physical satiety in the sense of having obtained sufficient physical release so that there is no possibility of more release apparently does not exist in women.

6. While cultural and psychological variables may make it difficult for a woman to experience either arousal or orgasm, physiologically it is a relatively easy matter to arouse a woman.

These findings run against the overwhelming weight of folk belief, cultural expectation, and the experience of most women. If it is no longer assumed that women don't need or want sex (and I suspect that many men and women are not yet ready to reject that assumption), it is still generally assumed that a woman's sexual needs are less than those of her husband and that she finds it much easier to control her sexual drive. In fact, however, the evidence suggests that a sexually aroused woman "can't help herself" in the sense that her body, once aroused, has both a powerful urge for satisfaction and the capacity for being aroused almost immediately once again. Uninhibited by cultural and psychological barriers, a woman's sexuality appears to be both more intense and more demanding than that of a man.

It is obvious that if a woman's sexuality is so powerful, tremendous cultural and psychological barriers have been built up not merely to contain such driving hunger but even to persuade most women that it does not exist. Such powerful constraints are bound to impede personality growth and cause moderate if not severe psychological harm.

It is not yet clear how restraints on female sexuality came to be, and given the fact that they appear to be very ancient (though there are tribes which do not have them), it may be impossible for us to ever know for certain. Some scholars have suggested that in the evolutionary process the female of the human species ended up with a physiology that left her at all times like the females of other primate species when they are in heat. A woman constantly capable of orgasm and insatiably demanding it would be a tremendous threat to the stability and peace of her tribe— and presumably also to her own health and welfare. As man evolved both biologically and culturally and began to organize himself, first into families and then into small agricultural villages, such sexuality became even more of a threat to the fragile structure he was trying to elaborate. It therefore became necessary to develop powerful inhibitions to control female sexuality. The fear of the female, so widespread in primitive tribes, and the powerful taboos imposed on sexuality in this view of things were amply justified by the threat that they presented to mankind's emerging social structure.

The point of view of some militant feminists, that man forced such cultural and psychological restraints on women, is historically and socially far too simple. (It is part of the standard contemporary political strategy of gaining a moral advantage over someone else by saying that as your predecessors oppressed my predecessors so you are victimizing me, and you should do penance by letting me victimize you for a while.) Presumably, men and women both benefited in many respects from a more stable and productive social order. Presumably, men and women both have had to pay a heavy price for the loss of sexual responsiveness in so many women down through the centuries. Presumably, too, an insatiable genitality over which social conventions exerted no control and which suffered no psychological restraints could make life very difficult for a woman.

The explanation is perhaps plausible and interesting, but scarcely documented beyond doubt and probably largely irrelevant to the present situation. The race is not about to return to the forests (there aren't many to return to, anyway). Most women are committed irrevocably to the family and are not going to be persuaded that promiscuity will solve any of their problems. Nor, if the truth be told, are there many women who would think that fifty orgasms an hour is an appropriate goal. Indeed, considerable numbers of them would be satisfied with just one. Whatever explanations we may finally settle on about the origins of the restraints on female genitality, the problem in our day is not to eliminate the restraints completely but rather to facilitate the development of a more healthy and more open attitude toward sex in as many women as possible.

It is clear, then, that a woman's sexuality is a very powerful force when she is aroused. Society and culture have not only imposed necessary restraints on female sexuality but have caused an overreaction to such an extent that many women experience little if any sexual pleasure.

We must be wary about such generalizations. It is altogether possible that many more women have in fact achieved healthy levels of genital satisfaction than are willing to talk about it. The cultural restraints may have applied only to discussion and not to experience. Most of the anthropological literature about Ireland, for example, describes it as a sexually repressed nation, yet one need only read the folk tales and poetry translated from Gaelic to realize that there was a very bawdy component to Irish culture.

We are thus entering a period of change when women's sexual hunger and sexual satisfaction are both more acceptable and more expected. For most women this will present a dilemma. Intense sexual pleasure is now all right, but how does one go about experiencing it? In other words, orgasm is now not only the object of legitimate pursuit but also something of an obligation. However enlightened they may be in theory and however convinced by the research evidence that they are capable of sustained and intense sexual delight, women are still caught in the cultural norms of the past as well as their childhood and adolescent experiences. On the one hand, their intellects tell them that they should find out if it is really true that they are insatiable; and, on the other hand, emotional residues of the past warn them that such thoughts are shameful; then the new social application which makes orgasm compulsory demands that they overcome their awkwardness, their diffidence, and their shame instantaneously.

Most women will cope with this problem, if at all, in the marriage relationship. Some "experts" argue that it is debatable whether a context of friendship and love is necessary to develop a satisfactory genital relationship. They point out that the research evidence indicates that almost any man can bring a woman first to sexual arousal and then to repeated orgasm with a television camera grinding away in the background. But then, of course, most people do not make love in the presence of a TV camera, and most people do not have the powerful motivation for sexual success provided by the expectations of the people who are operating the camera. Orgasm, presumably, can take place with almost anyone, but given the fact that human beings endow their relationships with meaning, a satisfactory genital relationship for most of us will require a context of meaning. This context becomes even more important when one (or usually both) partner has a problem overcoming shame, inhibition, disgust, and fear.

But quite apart from the theoretical possibility that a

woman can achieve sexual pleasure in other relationships, the truth still remains that most women will experience orgasms in marriage or not at all. Hence the real problem is to improve understanding, insight, and skills—both physical and psychological—in the marriage relationship.

Even though the research of Masters and Johnson and others indicates an astonishing ignorance on the part of many men as to what it takes physiologically to arouse a woman, this part of the problem is relatively simple. If a man is ignorant of what it takes to arouse his wife, it is much to be feared that his ignorance is a matter of choice. Both fantasy and folklore make it perfectly clear what he ought to be doing. He has his hands, his mouth, his penis— what does he think they are for?

The young man on the beach whose fantasy is so eagerly removing the bikini from the girl passing by knows exactly where he wants to put his hands, and deep down in her personality, she knows where she wants his hands to be put and, for that matter, where she would like to put her hands on him. If they should become in due course genital lovers and if he has the courage to follow the inclinations of his fantasy, he will certainly not be very much off the appropriate target. He may need guidance from her as to exactly what he should be doing, but he will certainly know where to begin.

And yet in many cases he will not do so. He may be afraid to experiment, he may be put off by her immediate reaction, a shameful and terrified resistance. Both of them may be trapped in rigid, guilt-ridden morality, which makes them feel that the appropriate actions are "dirty." Perhaps most important of all, the two of them may be afraid to talk honestly and openly about their sexual needs and problems. The relationship goes on, they periodically have intercourse, children are born; but for all the explicit attention they pay to their lovemaking, particularly the question of the wife's satisfaction in the lovemaking, they might just as well not be married.

Conversation between men and women about their genital relationship, and particularly about how the two of them can achieve greater delight and pleasure from that relationship, presumes, at least in most cases, an atmosphere of trust, confidence, openness, and love. A woman can hardly tell a man that he is not doing enough to stimulate her unless she is reasonably confident that their love is strong enough so that the husband will not be permanently offended by such a threat to his masculinity. Nor can a man ask a woman whether he is doing "the right things" to her unless he is reasonably sure that there is enough affection between them for her to overcome her initial reluctance to respond to such frank questioning. There is no doubt that in our time there is less reluctance to talk about such things than there was in the past, although frequently (particularly in the intellectual or would-be intellectual segment of the population) talk in even clinical detail is merely a more subtle form of noncommunication. I am frequently surprised by how many married couples, often after many years of rather unsatisfactory genitality, are able to notably improve both the quality of their sex lives and the whole atmosphere of their marriage after only a few conversations. There is no substitute in marriage for a wife who periodically plays the active and aggressive role in lovemaking, but neither is there any substitute for a man's making absolutely sure that his wife does not feel cheated or exploited—especially since so many women become so skillful at faking satisfaction rather than admit to their husbands that all is not as exciting as it should be.

If even some of the research on feminine sexuality is true (and there is little reason to doubt it), we must conclude that there is a fantastic amount of sexual frustration among American women—some of it no doubt perceived as sexual frustration, much more of it vague and undefined. The frustration is probably even worse for those wives who have read enough to know that they should be enjoying sex, but who are caught in patterns of genitality with their husbands in which they either pretend not to be especially interested in sex or pretend to orgasms they never experience.

A woman has one advantage: unless she is completely insensitive to her husband's reactions, she knows exactly what it takes to arouse him to the heights of sexual passion. She may never use this knowledge, but she always has it to use if she chooses.

Yet her task is still complicated and difficult. In addition to all her other responsibilities she must engage in a semipermanent seduction of her husband if she is to win the war for his attention from his career. She must overcome his subliminal fears about being an unskilled and inadequate lover—fears which beset many American men. She must teach him the combination of psychological tenderness and physical directness that are absolutely essential if he is to satisfy her. She must bluntly and explicitly guide him to refined knowledge about her physiology. If he is to be an adequate lover, she must make him one—and all the time maintaining an atmosphere that suggests that he is more than adequate, although both of them may know that he is not.

It is not fair that a woman should have to do all of these things. It is not fair that she must assume the responsibility for training her husband to be a lover while letting him think that he is initiating her into the joys of sexuality. But it is much to be feared that in our culture the only alternative for most women is continued sexual frustration.

These facts were made quite clear to me by a couple in their late thirties whom I had known very well. They had married early and produced a brood of children. He was a well-meaning, sincere, and very successful businessman whose knowledge of the physiology and psychology of women was practically nonexistent. He was very sorry about the "emotional problems" his wife had, but he was quite incapable of linking them with sexual frustration, much less with his inadequacies as a lover. Nor, when their marriage began to come apart, could he understand what was going on. When a friend suggested to him that his wife was hungry for attention and affection (and they might have added tenderness and orgasm), he was utterly baffled. He was a good husband and father, he worked hard, paid all the bills, provided clothes, cars, a home, vacations, educations. What more could he do?

I do not think he "played around" with other women, although many men in his situation do. Deciding that fulfillment of sexual fantasies can't happen in marriage, many men (and women) look elsewhere for their "kicks." They feel guilty about their infidelity, but never think that it may be their fault when there are no "kicks" on the marriage bed. In this case, there were many other aspects of the collapse of the marriage, but the genital relationship was both a partial cause of the other problems and a symbol of everything that had gone wrong with their marriage.

After considerable excellent therapy the woman decided that she wanted to save the marriage because of the children and, as she put it, "I still like the goof." In a conversation with me, she described the "long talk" she was going to have with him as a beginning of their reconciliation. I knew them both well and cared deeply about them, so I decided to set aside my sense of delicacy (or perhaps my Irish prudery) to speak bluntly. I observed that a reconciliation meant not a long talk but the renewal of a love affair—or, in their case, the beginning of the love affair which their marriage had only pretended to. "And," I concluded, "love affairs don't begin with long talks."

She agreed that they did not. "What do they begin with?"

"They begin with seduction."

She smiled somewhat ruefully. "I could pick him up at the train station tonight and have him seduced in about thirty seconds."

"Have you ever?"

Of course she had not. She realized that it was not the only problem in their marriage, but she also knew enough from her therapy to know that seducing her husband fairly often was an essential prerequisite for saving the marriage —and had been one of the indispensable missing ingredients in their previous relationship.

Only in part was she uncertain about her physical attractiveness as a woman. The major difficulty was that she was unsure how she would be able to cope with the new forces and the new vulnerability in their marriage that seducing her husband in the automobile would introduce— particularly if similar behavior became a frequent part of her life.

It was certainly "unfair" that she was in the position where she had to take all the risk and assume all the burden of beginning to stitch the relationship back together. It was "unfair" that she had to be the first one to put aside the vast amount of residual prudery that remained in their relationship. It was "unfair" that she had to be the first one to make herself radically vulnerable. Perhaps in the future of Western culture this injustice will be done away with. But if this woman wanted a passionate lover for a husband, she had no choice but to accept the unfairness of the situation and drive her car to the railroad station.

She didn't that day. But she did eventually, and as far as I can see, she doesn't seem to regret it.

There are, of course, some—perhaps many—instances in which a woman will need some sort of therapeutic help before she can enjoy sex. In other cases, a man who has not made it his business to discover precisely what it takes to make his wife writhe in uncontrollable joy is not much of a man. He takes his sex when and if he can get it, which is a coward's way out. A man can think of himself as a successful lover only when his wife wants him as badly as he wants her. Indeed, if we are to believe the recent researchers on female sexuality, the truly successful male lover will have succeeded in arousing his wife to such a point that she habitually wants him more than he wants her; and since most men want their women with barely controllable passion as often as possible, the thought that they could want them even more passionately should open up vistas of endless pleasure and delight. (To quote Hamlet out of context, "Tis a consummation devoutly to be wished.")

If so few lovers enjoy such pleasure, the reason may very well be that so few of them want it badly enough to take the risks involved: those of breaking away from shame, reticence, timidity, and fear.

6

The Uncertain Male

A recent article in the *New York Times* quoted a number of psychiatrists as reporting an alarming increase in the number of cases of male impotency. The psychiatrists hypothesized that the cause might be the increased demand for sexual fulfillment from "liberated" women. Such demands, the psychiatrists theorized, might frighten even more men who are already troubled by their own feelings of sexual inadequacy. One very obvious way for a man to escape from the insistent sexual demands of a woman who frightens him is to withdraw from the sexual fray altogether by becoming impotent.

In addition, the ideal of "human liberation" pushed by the women's movement can be terribly threatening to a man, not merely because it challenges his already precarious feeling of superiority, but also because he sees his woman seeking for a form of freedom, creativity, and spontaneity that is denied him by the social structure and culture as much as it used to be denied her. If he were any kind of a man at all, he must think, he would be pursuing the same goals of freedom which she is pursuing.

New York is not the rest of the country, and the offices of New York psychiatrists may not be the best sampling points in the nation. The

115

number of cases of psychological impotency may not be increasing. But the New York report merely serves to emphasize something that is well known but rarely discussed—the sexual uncertainties and inadequacies of American males.

The popular myth sees women as more afraid of sex than men; fear of the wedding night trauma, shame over physical nakedness, disgust with intercourse, frigidity, slowness to sexual arousal, all these are cited as evidence that women are, to say the least, sexually "slower" than men—despite the data cited in the previous chapter.

Physiological arousal does come more quickly for a man than a woman, not much more quickly perhaps, but somewhat more, and in that "somewhat" there is a considerable difference between man and woman. The average healthy man can get an erection very quickly and experience an orgasm after a very brief period of stimulation—much too brief from the viewpoint of his woman. If all sex was about was erection and orgasm, sexual problems of men would be very few indeed.

But since humankind is a self-conscious, self-reflective, interpreting creature there are other problems for male sexuality, and the very quickness with which man can become aroused can be a serious liability. A man's sexual need and desire is physically obvious. He cannot conceal an erect penis very well nor can he explain it away as the result of cold as a woman can account for hardened nipples. It is clear that a man with an erection has, for the moment at least, most of his physical and psychological resources invested in that erection. The irresistible need to do something about it has taken possession of him. He has lost the dignity, self-control, and restraint that comes from being the complete master of his passions. Quite simply, his whole personality wants a vagina and wants it quickly, and there's not much he can do to hide this fact.

But he can be rejected. That which his penis seeks can be denied him, and there is nothing more ludicrous or foolish than a sexually aroused male who is turned down. He has exposed his maleness and it has not been deemed good enough. He has made a fool of himself and there is no way he can conceal the fact.

(Women sometimes report how humiliated they feel when they take the sexual initiative and get no response. As one woman put it, "It is infuriating to go through the whole seduction scene and then be told that he is tired and has a headache and doesn't feel up to it." At least in some cases, there is little reason to doubt that the man is deliberately and not altogether unconsciously trying to show his woman what it is like to experience doubt and uncertainty *every time* you begin a sexual encounter.)

The fear of a failure is an abiding part of the sexuality of many, if not most American males. There are, of course, a tiny fraction of men who have problems with physiological impotency in their younger years. A considerably larger group have occasional, intermittent or frequent problems of psychological impotency, mostly rooted in a combination of fear and the need to punish. But many, many more men are harrassed at the semiconscious level with a fear of impotency and the related feeling of woeful inadequacy as a lover. What if one finds oneself naked in the presence of a sexually aroused and desirable woman and then is simply unable to get an erection? How utterly contemptuous she will be and how foolish and worthless he will seem. Or what if one does a poor job—a quick erection, a hasty and fleeting experience of intense pleasure and then the man lies spent while the woman reflects with disgust on how bumbling and incompetent he is as a sexual partner?

Most women, I suspect, are not at all aware of how strong these fears are in their men and many men permit themselves only dimly to face these fears. Yet, psychiatrists, psychologists, and marriage counselors will insist that such fears are, if not universal, at least pervasive in the society.

In a culture like ours, the position of the male is at best precarious. He is expected really to be two different persons. In the world of career, he is supposed to be vigorous, hard-driving, ruthless, ambitious, committed to success ("instrumental" or "agentic," to use the words of psychologists). On the other hand, when he goes into the family psychological environment he is expected to be gentle, compassionate, tender, sympathetic ("expressive" or "communal," to use the opposite psychological terms). He learned these latter skills more or less adequately as a child but always with the realization that when he grew up and became a man he would have to shed them in order that he might begin the struggle for "success." Thus, he was never permitted to be easy in the communal skills as a child, not nearly as easy and relaxed in them as was his sister, and in the years of adolescence and youth he was forced to go through the trauma of acquiring agentic and instrumental skills whether he wanted to or not. Small wonder that he felt guilty about the expressive dimensions of his personality and also feared that they might cripple him in the struggle for success.

In other words, in the world of profession, career and job, a man is forced to be agentic even though he has little confidence in his abilities in this direction; and in his relationship with his wife and family, he is expected to be communal even though he has little confidence in these skills either. To make matters worse, occupational success is taken in our society to be a proof of masculinity. You prove your virility in one way in the world in which you work and in a quite different way in the marriage bed and at the dinner table. The usual unsatisfactory compromise is something that is not agentic enough for the world of career and not expressive enough for love making. The man approaches his wife like she is a client to whom something must be sold, realizing probably that this is not the way to do it, but not knowing for sure what he should be doing. If you are a virile man, argues the reasoning behind this compromise, a woman will find you irresistible and all you need to do is take her. The net result is a male who in the genital encounter is neither agentic enough nor communal enough. He does not know either when to be strong or when to be weak, or how to take, or how to permit himself to be taken, and you really cannot be virile unless you can combine the expressive with the instrumental. The "stud" may "ball" a woman but that's all he can do. The virile man, on the other hand, knows how to make love, knows how to combine aggressiveness with tenderness, demand with surrender.

No matter how much they may deceive themselves by the locker room version of masculinity, most men know this is the case, and hence feel inadequate when it comes to lovemaking. They will presumably have both an erection and orgasm in the next sexual encounter but they know that they still very likely will do it "all wrong." There is a difference, the man knows, between a firm, passionate, demanding lover and someone who merely wants to be "laid." A man may pretend that they are the same thing but deep down he knows better.

The man's virility, then, is put to test in the success world and found inadequate—at least by his own very high standards—because he isn't tough enough, and it is also put to the test in bed where it is both too tough and not tough enough—and always at the wrong times. How does one read a woman's signals, how does one know when to push ahead, when to brush aside defenses that are not seriously meant, when to tread carefully, when to be gentle, and when to be fierce. A man's reaction is some version of "damned if I know."

The result for many men is that they take sex when they can get it, when their women dole it out to them. A few moments of passion and tension release followed by semiconscious feelings of frustration and inadequacy. And women, partly as punishment of inadequate lovers and partly for self-defense, become very good at doling out sex in such a way as to guarantee that their men continue to feel inadequate as lovers.

In addition, for all their fierce braggadocio, men are afraid of women, a fear that goes beyond the mere fact that a woman can reject them and can maintain the appearances of sexual coolness and control when they are clearly and defenselessly aroused—though that fear is bad enough. In the very earliest years of life a little boy is warned not to be like a little girl and is under constraint not to associate too closely with little girls lest they capture him and make him like them. Similarly, while he is expected to feel great tenderness for his mother, he is also warned that it is necessary to break away from her "apron strings" in order to become a man. In other words, if you permit yourself to be too closely involved with women and too dependent on them they may take your masculinity away.

Freudian psychoanalysts refer to this as a castration fear and there can be no doubt that for some men this fear of a loss of masculinity to castrating women is very powerful and very literal. But even where the symbol does not become that explicit the fear of being "too close" to a woman is still powerful. A man learns early in life that the safest way to deal with a woman is to be self-possessed, a bit aloof, only partially involved. He must keep his options open, certainly psychologically, and perhaps physically, too, and he must also maintain a veneer of mastery, self-confidence, and strength; he may need periodic sexual satisfaction from a woman, and he may also want a wife, but he still must maintain the image to her and to himself and to outside observers that he is not overly involved with her and can be, if he wants, independent of her.

But in fact, his real needs are much different and much more primal for, like all humans, he needs to be both "mothered" and wanted. His wife needs to be "mothered," too, but perhaps not as much as he does, because she learned early in life much better than he did how to both solicit and receive affection. To be "mothered" means to be smothered with affection, to be covered with sensuous attention, to have every part of one's being, body, and spirit gently and passionately caressed, to experience a relationship which furnishes the psychological equivalent of a hot bath and a warm, dry robe after coming in out of a cold, damp rainstorm. Mothering is, of course, a powerfully sexual activity, both between actual mother and child and between adults who provide an ambience of psychic warmth for each other. It is not merely physiological, but the physiological component of mothering is essential. A child needs to be physically caressed and the child in all of us needs periodic opportunities to assert itself and luxuriate in the warmth of physical touch. Orgasm may be the conclusion of such a caressing experience (though it need not), but the caressing experience is important in itself and not merely as a prelude to orgasm.

One young man I knew complained constantly that his wife did not "encourage" him enough. She understood this to mean that she did not exhort him enough to business and professional success so she redoubled efforts in that direction which were already more than adequate. Nor did he really need that she should be available for intercourse. She surely was ready for that and perhaps more ready than he was. What he meant, though he didn't know how to say it, and would have been afraid to if he did, was that he needed frequent, if not constant, psychological and physical caressing from his wife. She could not have mothered him too much—an observation which can be made about most women in their relationship to their men. There is no upper limit to the amount of caressing a man can absorb. The more the better. And the more direct and physical and sensuous—and if you wish, "obscene"—the caressing is, the better it will be. Does a man need to be "aroused"? In the physiological sense, generally he does not. He can have an erection merely at the sight of a woman's beginning to unbutton her dress, and he can have an orgasm with only the most passive acquiescence from her body. But in a psychological sense, man desperately needs to be aroused. He can be confident enough of his selfhood, his masculinity, his skills as a lover only when the woman has put considerable effort into building his morale, to reassuring him of his work, and encouraging him in his skills. She does not need to caress him in order to have intercourse, but she needs to show him constant affection, to build a psychological atmosphere in which he is self-confident enough to be a lover. He can only be expressive and communal when the strength of her expressiveness makes it difficult, if not impossible, for him to be anything else. The experience of being mothered, then, is absolutely essential for most men in order that they might become confident about their adequacies and strength as men.

And closely related, indeed simply another aspect of "mothering," is a man's need to be wanted. He becomes free to be an imaginative, liberated lover when he perceives that his wife wants him as much as he wants her. It is difficult for many women to convey such a desire to men. Physiologically, their sexual arousal is easier to hide;

psychologically, they have been trained to conceal their sexual desires and to keep men at bay by a relative indifference to sex. Their man seems confident enough, though his confidence does not make him particularly satisfactory at responding to her deep needs, but why should she take the risk of admitting to herself and him that she craves sexual union as much as he does.

And yet, the uncertain, hesitant male keeps wondering how good he is and his confidence in his own sexuality grows as he sees his wife become more and more quickly aroused by him. She does obviously and clearly hunger for him. He really does "turn her on" consistently and not intermittently (and the failure of many women's attempts to become sexually aggressive is that they are not consistent). One can take it as almost axiomatic that a man will not become a skillful lover until it becomes obvious to him that his wife hungers for his body, for, in perceiving that hunger, he perceives, perhaps for the first time, his worth as a male sexual creature.

Being mothered and being wanted can be discussed separately but in a man's life they are inextricably linked. His wife's affection conveys to him both his goodness and lovability as a male human and also her desire for him. For all their pretense at strength, rationality, vigor, and efficiency, there are few men who do not yearn for the sensual attention of some woman who can simultaneously mother and seduce them. The folk wisdom says that the male must arouse the female, and in a certain physiological sense, this is true. But if arousal means, not merely stimulation of erectile tissues, but also the development of confidence in one's expressive capacities and in the blend of agency and communion in one's personality, then the exact opposite is the case. It is, in most circumstances, the woman who must arouse the man.

At one level of consciousness, most women know that

they have been superbly designed to help their husband become more confident of his maleness. Every inch of a woman's body can be a joy to a sexual partner, not merely in intercourse or its immediate prelude, but in the whole ambience of their lives. In her fantasy life, a woman knows that she can turn her man's existence into a never-ending experience of sensual delight, but in reality she is much more hesitant, in part because of culturally induced shame, but in greater part because of the radical exposure of self, both physically and psychologically, that such an approach to the relationship would involve. What if he rejects her advances? What if he refuses to be caressed? What if he does not want to be wanted, or does not want to be mothered? The point is that on occasion he will, if only because a woman bent on keeping her husband in a semipermanent state of sexual arousal will frighten most men, at least occasionally. What she needs is confidence that she is good enough to break through his rejection.

However good they may be at manipulating a man's fears and insecurities, most women do not even begin to comprehend how fragile their husband's sexual egos are and how deeply they need the most obvious kinds of affection and reassurance. It is a rare woman who can say to herself, "Culture and upbringing have made him more afraid of me and of lovemaking than I am of him. Every sexual encounter between us is more of a risk for him than it is for me." And yet, in most relationships, the beginning of wisdom for a woman is to face and accept these truths.

What can a man do? He cannot talk to other men about his fears of sexual inadequacy. He is afraid to talk to his wife about it for fear she will ridicule him. He may seek out a psychiatrist, though few men do, and he may become impotent to punish his wife, though even fewer men do that. On balance, then, there is little for him to do but suffer through a life of very incomplete and inadequate sex, experiencing orgasm with decreasing satisfaction, and wondering why it seems so trivial much of the time.

Ultimately, there is no escape from such a fate unless a man is able to face his own needs to be mothered and to be wanted, admit them to himself, and then share them with his wife. Such an act of sharing may well be the critical episode in their sexual life. If she ridicules him or is frightened or tries to change the subject or refuses to understand what he is saying then he surely will never mention it again. If, on the other hand, she is capable of being sensitive, compassionate, understanding, and affectionate, a whole new dimension of their sexual life may begin, for her husband will then realize that she respects him, not less but more, because he can talk about his fears and weaknesses and uncertainties. He will understand, not merely in theory but in warm and passionate reality, that a man who can admit his uncertainties and his fears is not less a man but more a man than the one who cannot. A man who can yield himself to a woman in utter defenselessness is not a weakling or a coward or someone who is asking to be castrated but a strong, confident man who knows that his masculinity will survive no matter what the exposure of weakness and fear may lead to. A woman who does not admire and respect such a man, who does not want to link her body with his as quickly as possible is a failure as a woman and as a human being. But, of course, one puts the whole relationship in jeopardy by even raising such a question.

How, then, does a man find the strength he needs to plead for tenderness, affection, reassurance, constant caressing; how does he work up the courage to tell his wife that he needs to be wanted; how does he come by the virility that is required to give himself over to the care of a woman in a way analogous to that by which a little boy surrenders to his mother? This question, I would submit, like all the other difficult questions raised in this volume, is fundamentally a religious one because it asks how much one can trust reality, whether the universe is gracious and benign to risk-takers or whether the wise and prudent man avoids risk-taking, even though the payoff may be great. A man discussing his sexual uncertainties with his wife represents not merely an act of faith in her and in himself but in reality, whether one spells it with a small r or a capital R. That few men are able to take this risk suggests that there are only few men who are convinced that reality is gracious enough to underwrite such exposure of self. The religious dimension of this exposure of sexual uncertainty may not be explicit, though religious symbols are not very good if an exploration of their meaning does not reveal some insight that strengthens a man's resolve to let his woman see him as he really is.

In the Christian symbol system, the most obvious proof that one does not lose masculinity or strength by exposing one's needs and desires is to be found in Yahweh making it quite clear how desperately he wants to be loved by his people, and making it clear indeed in explicitly sexual language. If Yahweh can admit that he "needs" the affection of his beloved, then why should any man be afraid to admit the same thing? And if Jesus could weep over Jerusalem because he so desperately wanted the response of that city, would it be a weak man who would weep as he tells his wife how much he needs to be wanted by her? It is hard for a man to concede his vulnerability, to put aside the pose of someone who is always in control of everything, but if God can concede his vulnerability, maybe the admission of vulnerability is a sign of strength and not of weakness.

If most men, troubled, at least in a small part of the back of their minds by their sexual insecurities and uncertainties, do not turn to such obvious religious symbols for strength, encouragement, and reassurance, the reason certainly in part is that the sexual implications of the religious symbols have been so long ignored (despite the fact that sexual imagery is pervasive in the Scriptures) and in part because sexual risk-taking, underpinned by profound and clearly thought out religious convictions would involve conversion of one's whole style of life. The ultimate issue, then, is more religious than sexual. Can we afford to take the risk that reality is good? Neither the insatiable female nor the uncertain male is at all certain that such a risk is justified. So their bed tonight is likely to be passionless or, if there is any passion, it will be episodic and transient. Technically, perhaps, orgasm has occurred for both of them but in that orgasm they perceive, however dimly, that something much better was possible, but somehow missed.

7

Sexual Intimacy and Children

Where do children fit into the sexual intimacy of their parents? The implication behind this question is that children are somehow an obstacle to the playful and passionate lovemaking of their parents; children either as a possibility or as a reality are a potential intrusion of the joys of intimacy.

It is argued that for a woman the fear of pregnancy is always a factor to be considered in lovemaking even if she is using contraceptives. When one wants a child or another child this fear is not important (though the discomfort and dangers of pregnancy are still something that will be on her mind). But if no more children are wanted, then fear of pregnancy is bound to inhibit a woman's spontaneity and joy when she enters a sexual encounter. If in addition she is a Catholic, she may be plagued by such guilt feelings that she cannot enjoy intercourse or indeed anything that seems even remotely related to it.

One must sympathize with those who are caught in such fear and guilt and one must acknowledge that they are both widespread. But about the cause of the fear, at least, nothing can be done. For most women in the fertile years of life, the possibility of pregnancy is always present, however limited the most effective contraceptives may make it. Short of sterilization there will always be a remote possibility of conception. But human existence itself is filled with dangers. It is risky to cross a street, but most people still cross streets. It is dangerous to drive an automobile, but few of us refuse to drive a car. There are some minor elements of risk in air travel, but it is generally acknowledged that fears of such travel are disproportionate to the danger. In other words, if fear of real but minor dangers keeps us from an ordinary human life, we may have a major psychological and religious problem, but that problem is not specifically sexual. If the existential biological fact that one's body is capable of conceiving a child prevents one from enjoying sex, then one surely needs help, but it does not follow that one's fears are natural or healthy or constitute a valid excuse for rejecting all but the minimum possibilities in sexual intimacy.

About the guilt of Catholics using contraceptives little can be said, since this book explicitly and deliberately intends to avoid the current moral debates within Catholicism (in the belief that the issues under debate can only be dealt with when adequate responses to the more fundamental questions raised in this volume are available). The research evidence is overwhelming that most Catholics use contraceptives and have convinced themselves that such use is not immoral. That there may be some residual uneasiness after such decisions is understandable. But if such unease becomes paralyzing even after a careful and conscious moral decision has been made in all good faith, then the problem is psychological, not ethical, and must be treated in the same way as any other psychological problem: when it interferes with normal human life, one needs competent professional help.

I do not intend to defend (or attack) the day-to-day sexual teaching of the Catholic church in the 1940s and the 1950s. That it caused hang-ups in some people cannot be questioned. On the other hand as a social scientist I must say that most of our general psychological and specifically sexual hang-ups come from our family experience and the church's teachings merely provide convenient reinforcement for problems which had already existed long before we came in contact with the church. The church can be faulted perhaps for not providing the religious vision which would support us in working our way out of our hang-ups. But scapegoating the church is a sign of emotional immaturity precisely because it is an escape from facing the real origins of problems in our family backgrounds.

A much larger question is the problem of the "intrusion" of children. One does not appear in sheer pantyhose and nothing else or begin proximate foreplay in the presence of children. One is not likely to engage in a night of passionate sexuality with a sick child in the house. One must make sure the door to the bedroom is tightly closed before one starts lovemaking—even if one has awakened in the middle of the night. In other words, when there are children in the house privacy means something quite different than it did when there were no children. Like it or not, there are more inhibitions on parental sexuality when children are present. The critical question is whether the man and woman permit these inhibitions to become controlling.

We live in a world of headaches, common colds, sick children, leaky faucets, broken car mufflers, uncertain air-conditioning units, winter snowstorms, late night telephone calls (to wrong numbers), insanely busy days, pests at the front door, and a thousand other harassments, annoyances and inconveniences. The question is not whether we can eliminate such distractions from our sexual intimacy or from our whole life experience. The question is rather whether we let them destroy our fundamental life serenity.

There are two ways to cope with the distractions, con- fusions and interruptions of our life. The normal way is to respond helplessly to them, to permit ourselves to be buffeted from demand to demand, from distraction to dis- traction, from annoyance to annoyance. Such a life is one of constant confusion and uncertainty, of wasted motion and mental exhaustion. But it has two distinct advantages: Having given ourselves over to the control of external forces we can argue that we are dispensed from personal responsibility. We can also point to our superior moral worth as evidenced by the exhaustion that results from trying to fulfill our multitudinous responsibilities.

In such a lifestyle children are of course an intrusion on sexual intimacy and so is everything else. Indeed, every- thing is an intrusion on everything else. It is a life, as James Thurber remarked, of noisy desperation.

The alternative lifestyle requires that one establish a hierarchy of goals and values and arrange one's life in such a way that distractions from high priority goals are reduced to a minimum. Planning, decisiveness, patience, and persistence are required to live this way—and prob- ably an extraordinary amount of self-confidence and self- control. In such a lifestyle, one is still not completely free from interruptions and distractions; but one has chosen to dominate and control the chaos of existence instead of be- ing dominated by it. Children may still intrude—for it is the nature of children to intrude. But parents organize their lives in such a way that there are times and places of guar- anteed privacy and other times and places of minimal like- lihood of distraction (even if this means occasional—or even frequent—trying to arrange a night together in a motel).

If one cannot organize one's life in such a way that sex- ual intimacy is a possibility, the problem is not in fact a sexual one at all but a larger psychological and religious one. If a man and woman say they are simply too busy with children and career to devote much time and attention to sex they are saying in effect that they have exercised certain options, even though the exercise may have been an implicit one covered up with a disguise of "responsibilities" and "obligations." If one chooses to be disorganized, chaotic, and confused, to be caught in a network of uncontrollable external "demands," then that is the choice one has made. But one then should blame oneself for the absence of anything more than casual sex in one's marital relationship and not the children for "intruding." In that case it is evident that one does not want an expanding sexual intimacy—at least not badly enough to take the decisive control of life that would be essential to make intimacy possible.

I am not suggesting that life can be programmed the way a computer can. The randomness of human events inevitably guarantees that all schedules go awry. A rigidly organized life is the opposite side of the coin of chaos. Both responses to the multiplicity of reality are attempts to avoid the need for mature choice in situations of conflicting demands. Order comes not from detailed schedules but from general guidelines and principles which are applied with ingenuity and flexibility. An organized life means not the absence of confusion but rather the ability to intelligently "play by ear" one's response to confusion —with the other ear listening to a clearly articulated set of values and goals. A lifestyle of control as opposed to a lifestyle of chaos does not mean that one wins all the battles. None of us are that mature, that self-disciplined. It merely means that we win more battles than we lose.

Or to put the matter more concretely: How much long-range planning does it take and how much money does it cost to guarantee a man and a woman a certain number of nights each year alone together with distractions short of disaster most unlikely? How much intelligence does it take to build into a year's schedule of such nights alternative dates in case the primary ones have to be canceled? Is the pay-off in their relationship worth the long-range planning and costs? It must be concluded that not all that much planning and not all that much money are involved. If a man and a woman say that they do not have the time or the money or the freedom to take such steps to facilitate the development of their fidelity and intimacy, then they either must claim that life is so harsh and cruel that they have been backed into a corner where sexual intimacy is impossible or they must admit that they have implicitly exercised options which have placed intimacy low on their list of priorities. One frequent option is to decide in effect that the pain and maturity necessary to exercise control over the chaos of existence is too heavy a price to pay for intimacy—or for any of the other benefits that the assumption of personal responsibility bestows.

The problem then is not the intrusion of children. The problem is rather choosing between responsible control over the circumstances of one's life or abdication of decisive, personal responsibility to the chaos of external demands. You pay your money and you make your choice. And it is a harsh existential reality that even not choosing is a choice.

In the short run, drifting is much easier than choosing. A life of response is easier than a life of responsibility. Blaming the environment is easier than asserting as much rational control as possible over the environment. Lamenting the absence of privacy is easier than taking the rational steps necessary to guarantee some privacy almost all the time and great privacy at least on occasion. Yielding to chaos is easier than imposing order on chaos. Hence it is not surprising that large numbers of people choose the former alternatives. There is great long-run pay-off in the latter alternatives but the costs of joining the battle for order and against chaos seem very high—and there is no absolute certainty of victory.

Does the Christian symbol system provide any illumination for the human dilemma of the struggle between order and chaos. The answer is so obvious as to seem almost trivial—except that it is rarely applied to the specific problem of personal responsibility and never to my knowledge to the problem of sexual intimacy.

Primitive man was greatly troubled by the disorder in the physical universe because the forces of chaos threatened his very existence. Storm, drought, disease, marauding enemies could easily sweep in on the tiny, fragile structure of his village or camp and destroy the supports of human existence over which he had labored so long. The social and physical structure of his village barely kept forces of chaos at bay even under the best possible circumstances. He therefore saw the conflict between order and chaos as the primal stuff out of which the world was created and pictured his gods as imposing some order on chaos in the act of creation—although the struggle between the gods and chaos was not definitively won and continued even in the present. Humans cooperated in the struggle on the side of the gods. Plowing the fields, building the village, watching the flocks were acts that shared in the creative activity of the gods because they represented the assertion of order over chaos. They became then necessarily religious acts and the religious rituals that celebrated the existence of the village and the cycle of fertility united man's ordering of his world with the cosmic ordering activity of the gods.

There is obviously a tremendous amount of this ordering cosmology in the book of Genesis. The Hebrews were as much concerned about the battle against chaos as were any of their desert neighbors. But if the setting of the conflict between cosmos and chaos is the same in the book of Genesis as it is in other creation myths, the actors are very different. Yahweh may get upset about the failure of his people to respond to his love, but he does not have much trouble with chaos. Yahweh does not struggle, he dominates. He is not locked in a difficult and almost equal battle; he eliminates chaos with a word. Ultimate victory is not in doubt; it has already been won. Man's work of ordering—represented by Adam's dominion over the garden and his naming of the animals—is not something that is required by the gods to continue the struggle against chaos. It is rather sharing in a victory which has already (in its basic outlines) been won.

One may choose not to believe the revelation contained in the religious symbolism of Genesis: the Ultimate Graciousness of Being has already triumphed over the forces of darkness, chaos and disorder and man's ordering activity is a way of sharing in victory. There is still much confusion and disorder—physical, social, and personal—in the cosmos. The revelation (or religious insight if you wish) in the Genesis Myth may seem too good to be true. It is not my purpose in this book to argue about the truth of the world view presented in the genesis symbolism, though I will assert that one can scarcely reject such a world view and make the claim to be Christian. My point is simply that if one believes the underlying religious truth of the genesis myth, one has very powerful motivation for exercising an option in favor of reasoned and rational personal responsibility over one's life. Chaos can be beaten; it is not necessary to surrender to the forces of confusion and disorder which swirl around us. We can choose, we can take control—at least up to a point. We can make decisions about what is important and what is not important. We can have privacy if it is important to us. Our struggle against the irrationalities and distractions of modern urban life are just as much a part of the ordering efforts of God as was primitive man's building the walls of his village and plowing his fields. The search for appropriate privacy and appropriate times is part of the ongoing battle of cosmos against chaos and we have Yahweh on our side. (The quest for privacy is obviously not the only dimension of the ordering struggle, but it is the one that is particularly the concern of this chapter.)

But is it not still too much to suggest that a man and woman who plan six months ahead of time for a day and a night in the privacy of a motel room in which they can give themselves over to the delights of sexual abandon are participating in God's creating and ordering activity (quite apart from whether any child is conceived during their interlude)? The old piety would dismiss such a notion as a shocking obscenity. The new cynics will dismiss it as religious romanticism. It may well be both. But if responsible personal control over the circumstances of one's existence is necessary for sexual intimacy to flourish and if the Genesis myth is precisely designed to underwrite the assumption of responsibility as an agent of order against disorder, of cosmos against chaos, then a powerful religious symbol system is available to re-enforce the search for privacy, should anyone wish to use the symbols. Religious symbols are options; they impose themselves on no one. If you don't believe the insight contained in the symbol, you don't have to. If you think that the insight is silly, you may say so. If you resent the use of the insight to underwrite the quest for sexual pleasure, that is a matter which is entirely up to you. Only don't say that the symbol is irrelevant to the problems of human life in general and sexual intimacy in particular. The potential for relevance is there if anyone wishes to use it. That the potential has been used but rarely in the past is not the fault of the symbol but of the potential users.

Do not complain to Yahweh, in other words, that the children he has sent you have so interfered with your privacy that satisfactory sex between you and your spouse has become impossible. For he might grow angry and send an angel to tell you to reread the first chapters of the book of Genesis.

The more important question about sexual intimacy and children is exactly the reverse of the one we have discussed in the previous pages: what impact does the sexual relationship of parents have on their children? That the question is asked so infrequently is evidence of how afraid of it most people are. Middle-class parents are willing to make every imaginable sacrifice to provide for the health and education of their children. Nothing is too important to be permitted to stand in the way of a college education. But far more important for a young person than going to college is growing up in a home where sexual intimacy between parents is healthy and growing. However, middle-class parents do their best to avoid facing this truth and try in effect to give their children the impression that physical genitality is something that really doesn't happen between them.

Until very recently the pretense that sex didn't exist between parents was so strong that nothing at all was said about sex and children learned the "facts of life" every place but in the home. More recently some parents (though by no means all or, one suspects, by no means even a majority) have been brave enough to communicate factual information—and if they are "liberal," a wealth of clinical detail—to their children. But few parents are willing to admit even to themselves that the atmosphere of sexuality in the home is immensely more important than "sex education" and usually speaks so loudly that the facts communicated in the frequently awkward "education" sessions are drowned out. Young people learn how to deal with sex by watching how their parents deal with it. The process may not be conscious or explicit (and usually is not) but there are countless cues every day as to what a man is and what a woman is and how they relate to one another. The children couldn't miss such cues even if they wanted to.

Two people who share the same house and the same bed and periodically join their bodies in the genital act (nine times a month on the average in the United States if we are to believe the survey researchers—who know everything) radiate an atmosphere about themselves that is almost palpable. The effects on their bodies and on their spirits of the abrasions and pleasures of their life together are powerful; the tangled network of cues and signs that they are constantly and habitually exchanging make it impossible for them to hide either the general quality of their relationship or the highly specific state of their activity on the marriage bed.

The atmosphere of a marriage is blatant and obvious to anyone who bothers to be sensitive to the cues between husband and wife. Most people train themselves to tune out the signals a marriage emits both because it is acutely embarrassing to witness a frustrating marriage and because if we examine the atmosphere of someone else's intimacy we must face the terribly painful fact that we too are exposing our intimacy for all to see.

Only the perverted would want to have others present when their naked bodies are linked either in warm and deep love or unsatisfactory and transient passion. But the "atmosphere" of a marriage makes clear to the world (or at least to those in the world who can't avoid the evidence) what goes in the marriage bed, just as though the genital act was taking place in public.

If the powerful and demanding sexual needs of the "insatiable female" are not being satisfied by her man, there is no way she can hide either the fact of his failure or her anger at it. Similarly, if the fears and insecurities of the "uncertain male" are getting worse instead of better, if his wife is making him more afraid of women rather than less, all the bravado and all the beer drinking in the world cannot hide his frustration. It is possible to go through a list of the couples one knows and separate those who clearly have fun in bed from those that clearly don't. Every married couple must realize that their friends can unerringly place them on one side of the list or the other, even if not a single word about sex has ever been said.

If the "atmosphere" of frustration or fulfillment is so clear to friends and even brief acquaintances, how absolutely overpowering it must be to children. If the sexual relationship between man and wife is mutually exciting and satisfying, the children know it, not explicitly or consciously perhaps, but in the depths of their personality. On the other hand, when their parents feel unsatisfied, cheated and angry over a dull and shabby sexual relationship, the children know it too and this knowledge will have a profound and potentially damaging impact on the children's own sexual development.

Psychiatrists have been telling us this for a long time, but more systematic social science has paid surprisingly little attention to the transmission of sexual role models across generational lines. An exception to this is my young colleague William McCready who calls his field of interest "the transmission of culture." In an ingenious piece of research, McCready has demonstrated the extremely close connection between religious socialization and sexual socialization: A young person learns his world view at the same time and in the same process as he learns his sexual identity. Indeed, McCready and his wife in an article in the January 1973 issue of *Concilium* have suggested that it is precisely the rigidity or expansiveness of one's definition of sexual identity that leads one to conclude very early in life that the world is either malign and arbitrary or benign and gracious.

If a child learns that there are certain kinds of behavior that are rigidly required of little girls and rigidly forbidden to little boys, it will be hard for him to believe that he lives in a benign and expansive universe. On the other hand if the child learns (from what his parents do and who they are far more from what they say) that the fully human person is a mixture of masculine and feminine, aggressive and tender, active and passive, dominant and submissive characteristics, he comes to believe—long before he acquires religious symbols—that he lives in a tolerant and gracious world where there is room for complexity and multiplicity, experimentation and risk-taking, openness and trust.

There is an inherent plausibility in the McCreadys' argument and they are now in the process of collecting data which will enable them to nail it down beyond reasonable doubt. Should they do so it will mean that faith and sexual identity are virtually the same thing.

But even before they get the kind of conclusive evidence which good social scientists demand, there can be little doubt that children learn both the fact and the components of their sexual identity and the appropriate style of relationships between the sexes from the atmosphere of the sexual relationship between their parents. What other models do they have to imitate? If being a woman does not mean being like mother, what does it mean? If being a man does not mean being like father, what can it mean? If playing the role of a husband means something else than the way father acts toward mother, what could it possibly be? And if being a wife means a different style of relationship with a man than the way mother behaves toward father, where is the child to learn this style?

If a woman deeply longs for the return of her husband
at the end of the day so that he can vigorously and joy
ously make her body come alive with passion and pleasure
both her son and her daughter will know—without her
ever having to say it—that things are well between mother
and father; and even though the full meaning of what goes
on may not be clear to the children for many years, their
mother's confident need for their father is superb prepara
tion for their own adult sexual relations.

Similarly if the son and daughter perceive, however
dimly, that father frequently caresses mother and that he
often wants to be alone with her the impact of the lesson
will not be lost on them.

Words, tone of voice, touches, quick smiles, secret
laughter, a flash of an eye, a twist of a hip, a brushing of
bodies, a meeting of hands, an occasional pinch, or pat or
squeal—all of these say far more to children than does the
most clinical and sophisticated "liberal" instruction (not
that instruction is out of place). If a man is sufficiently confident of his role as a masculine lover that he is able to
blend tenderness, passivity and gentleness into his personality and encourage his wife to be sexually aggressive, then
he says things about sex and maleness and femaleness to
his children that they will never forget. If a woman has
been reassured of her fundamental lovability as a woman
and if she has been sexually satisfied by her husband so
that she has no doubt about her own sexuality, if she can
mix into her personality components of vigor, forcefulness,
and aggression and can pursue her husband's body with at
least as much enthusiasm as that with which he pursues
hers, she will teach her children more about sex than they
could learn from all the sex education classes and all the
marriage manuals in the world (which is not to suggest
that classes and manuals do not have their own place).

Most men and women are not prepared to admit to themselves that often they use their children as a shield with which to protect themselves from both the terror and delights of intimacy. There are many different techniques for this particular kind of manipulation. "Obligations" to "the children" are cited as the excuse for permitting themselves little time alone with each other and even for allowing the marriage relationship to deteriorate through lack of care and attention. "The children" are frequently a woman's functional equivalent to a man's occupational responsibilities: both can easily be cited with self righteous feelings of virtue for paying little attention and devoting little time to the relationship between husband and wife.

Furthermore "the children" can be a justification for removing from the home environment all traces of eroticism save for those which may occur in the bedroom itself. And even in such connubial privacy weariness allegedly caused by "the children" or the possibility that they might stumble on the scene are used as a pretext for hasty, furtive and perfunctory lovemaking.

I once encountered what has always seemed to me a classic case of using the children as a protection against intimacy. A couple had undergone simultaneously a severe career crisis and a very difficult period in their personal and sexual relationship. The career crisis had been solved happily and they were going off to a quiet and very remote resort in tropic climes (it was winter) for a week of rest. But, even though their families were willing and even eager to take care of their two children, at the last moment it suddenly became absolutely essential that the children come along. The woman informed me that they had "neglected" the children during the crisis and now they had to "make it up" to them. Her husband was only too happy to agree. What had started out as a "second honeymoon" in which they would have had the freedom and the privacy for sensual experimentation that might have put their sexual relationship back on the tracks was converted—quite literally overnight—into an obligation to "the children" for, as the man called it, "a family vacation."

Of course it never occurred to them that they had a prior obligation to each other and that "the children" would benefit much more from having parents who were physically in love with each other than they would from five tense days under the sun. Or maybe it did occur to them, but they quickly shut such thoughts out of their minds.

And they resented what they had done. For part of both of them desperately wanted the time together for erotic play—and heaven knows they needed it. But they conspired with each other to deprive themselves of such time, blamed each other subliminally for what had happened, and spent most of the trip punishing each other, with the favorite form of punishment being accomplished through "the children." For there is not a parent in the world who does not know how (unconsciously at least) to make children irritable and thus punish his (or her) spouse.

What was unusual about this particular episode was not the technique itself but the fact that it was so ludicrously blatant. The man and woman were terrified of being alone with each other under circumstances where there would have been nothing else to do but make love. They had created a situation in which they would be trapped with each other and then when the chips were down used "the children" as an excuse for copping out. In fantasy they yearned for a "desert island" interlude. In real life, they fled it like it was a contagious disease.

The best sort of atmosphere for children to mature in is one in which their parents are engaged continually in seducing one another. Instead of the question being whether it is fair to the children for parents to devote considerable time and energy to developing their fidelity and intimacy the question is rather whether it is fair to the children not to. One makes love not because it is good for the children to do so but because it is a source of great delight and pleasure. Yet if one takes or is taken but rarely, there ought to be no doubt that the children will "know" however unconsciously, and that this knowledge cannot help but harm them. (It should be noted in passing that human nature is remarkably resilient. A child can grow up in the most rigid and frigid home and still achieve sufficient sexual maturity to have a happy relationship with a member of the opposite sex—sometimes. But what we are discussing here is not the capacity of the durable human offspring to survive the mistakes of its parents, but the ideal environment for sexual maturation.)

The sexual atmosphere of the home, present and past, is particularly critical when the child experiences the trauma of awakening adolescent sexuality. There comes a night when a girl lies in bed and realizes for the first time (consciously at least) that it is altogether possible that at this very moment her mother and father are engaging in sexual intercourse. If the atmosphere of the family is marked by constant efforts to pretend there is no sexuality in the house and by repressed sexual dissatisfaction and anger, this realization will come as a horrible shock to the girl. The union between the bodies of her parents will seem unspeakably ugly and dirty. If on the other hand the atmosphere of the sexual relationship between her mother and father has always been warm and tender, the girl will still be shocked but the shock will be a pleasant one. She will like her mother and father more not less and—this is critically important for an adolescent—she will like herself more. If her parents have the same feelings she has, then the feelings cannot be wrong and there is no need to worry about them. On the contrary, she can look forward to the day when she can engage in intercourse with her husband, because if her mother does it, it cannot possibly be dirty.

Similarly, the night will come when a young man sees in fantasy for the first time his father making love to his mother. If the atmosphere of his family experience tells him that sex is evil or that it does not really exist or that it is a constant unsatisfying war, he is likely to be violently angry at his mother and his father for being so vile and at himself, both for thinking of the vileness and for not being able to do anything about it. On the other hand, if the sexual electricity between his mother and his father has permeated the home in which he grew up, the boy will be delighted. For if his father can be attracted by his mother's body and if she not merely tolerates but enjoys his attention, then there is nothing evil or unnatural or shameful about his finding the bodies of his female schoolmates a source of constant fascination. And he can look forward with confidence and reasonable patience to the day when he too makes love to one of them.

But there is more to the sexual crisis of adolescence than coming to terms with one's dramatic new bodily feelings. It is essential to know that the feelings are not abnormal or foul. It then becomes necessary to know what to do with them. The adolescent needs an interpretation of his sexuality more than anyone else precisely because he has just discovered it. Sexual rebellion and experimentation among adolescents (and neither phenomenon was invented in 1973) are in fact a covert search for meaning. If a person can't believe what his parents or teachers or church tell him about sexuality, the only way he can find out what it means is by trying it himself (or herself).

Unfortunately young people frequently have good reason for not trusting their elders. For parents (and church and school) have not told them the truth. But worst of all, there has been nothing in the attitudes and behavior of parents toward each other to indicate that they have a coherent system of values which enables them to enjoy the fullness of their sexual passions and energies.

Or to put the matter the other way round, if it is clear that the parents have obtained great enjoyment and satisfaction from their own sexual relationship, the children are perfectly willing and indeed eager to find out what their values are—how they have managed it when so many others have failed. If, on the other hand, it is evident to the children that their parents don't make love all that often, and don't enjoy it that much when they do, there doesn't seem to be any really good reason why they should listen to their parents telling them what is right and what is wrong.

It is as simple as that. All the rules, lectures, warnings and temper tantrums in the world are no substitute for a mother and father who still obviously enjoy going to their bedroom every night. If mother has frequently come down to breakfast in the morning with a special glow, then her son and daughter will listen to her when she talks about sex and marriage. And if father is still obviously intrigued by the wonders of his wife's body he will have no trouble getting his children's attention when he begins to pontificate about sex. He may talk like Polonius but his offspring know that he does not live that way and that he can do much better things than talk when he is alone with his wife.

There is great chaos and confusion in the sexual lives of adolescents and young people—maybe no more than in the past, but surely more than enough. One of the main reasons for the chaos is that only a very few young people grow up in the sexual atmosphere described in the previous paragraph. It is another example of the struggle between cosmos and chaos, between order, value and responsibility on the one hand—disorder, normlessness, and surrender to external pressures on the other. One must order one's own life to enjoy intimacy and fidelity; but having created an atmosphere in one's home that is suffused with a healthy and passionate sexuality, one thereby equips one's children with the attitudes and values which are the raw materials by which they can create cosmos in the midst of the chaos they will experience in their own lives.

One does not love one's mate or lust after the mate's body because it is good for the children—not at least unless one is sicker than even most of the denizens of middle-class society are. A man does not look down his wife's dress and pat her buttock or pinch her thigh when these parts of her anatomy are conveniently present because such actions are good example for his children. He does these things because they are the obvious thing to do. When they cease to be obvious to him and to his wife, however, the children are going to miss a critically important part of their education.

Nor does a woman keep her body in trim, play with her husband's hair, or make the morning and evening kiss a promise and an invitation because such behavior is good for her children. But if she has lost interest in these fundamentals of seduction, her children are being cheated of something that they have a right to: a mother who is not afraid to show that she thinks it's fun to seduce her husband.

8

Sex and Conflict

We live imperfect lives in an imperfect world. Our friendships lack elegance and grace in their self-revelation. Some misread the cues from their lovers. The taking is sometimes too crude and sometimes too timid. The yielding is frequently begrudging and reluctant. The lovemaking is often inept and insensitive. Weariness, nervousness, "headaches," distractions, to say nothing of fear, anxiety and neurotic regression, all inhibit the generosity of our friendship and the free-flowing of sexual energies. Even the most passionate and skillful of lovers, even the most trusting and confident of friends know that in many of their encounters the balance of satisfaction over frustration is thin, and married lovers often fall off into sleep after their bodies have separated angry at themselves and at each other for what they know was an inexcusably pedestrian performance.

One of the ways in which love grows is by conflict. Such a statement obviously runs against much of the romanticism about love. An "ideal marriage" is one in which the lovers never fight, but beware of the couple which proudly proclaims that they have never quarreled, for either their relationship involves immense amounts of repression or they are archangels.

Lovers must fight. They can only love if they fight; it enhances the quality of their love. Love without conflict is tame, passionless, dull.

In intimacy, powerful forces are released, forces that blend immense psychic and physical intensity. The integration of the genital and psychic needs of two people is an extraordinarily difficult task, because neither individual has anything but limited control over his emotions and hungers. Within intimacy, each must understand and to some extent adjust not only his own hungers and needs but also the hungers and needs of his partner. Love is not the successful accomplishment of a balance among all these surging passionate forces; it is rather the constant effort to strive for a temporary integration of the forces, which will be a prelude to yet more effort. No realistic lovers think that any balance will be permanent, and all passionate lovers know that finding a balance, however transitory, is one of the great joys of their love.

Conflict is an absolutely indispensable mechanism for growth in intimacy. It is the way two lovers disclose to one another the "imperfect fit" in their physical and psychological needs. It is a means for disclosing to each other aspects of their personalities that have previously been hidden. It not merely releases the inevitable tensions that build up in a shared life. It is also a manifestation of love, for conflict between lovers is a means by which they say to one another, in effect, that their love and trust is so great that they are not afraid to reveal to each other their anger and they have no need to hide the raw edges of their personalities.

The most obvious—and the most simple—form of marital conflict is over genitality. Let's say that the husband, for example, is one of those blessed human beings who awakens after six hour's sleep relaxed, refreshed, and instantly ready to face the challenges of the day. Upon awakening he becomes intensely conscious of his wife sleeping quietly and peacefully beside him. She may be a bit bedraggled—as everyone is in the early morning—but in the soft light of morning she seems almost unbearably desirable. He wants her and he wants her now. What better way to begin the day than with a little lovemaking. Sex before breakfast? A fantasy he dreamed of before marriage and one that he can now legitimately fulfill.

What he doesn't know is that his wife, like much of the rest of the human race, is not really capable of human behavior until she has had her third cup of coffee. It is not merely that she objects to sex at 5:00 a.m.; she objects to anything at that hour. She doesn't loathe her husband particularly at that time of the morning—no more than she would loathe the alarm clock, for which she feels a deep and abiding hatred.

Both people knew before they married that not everyone reacts to the early morning in the same way. Both realized that their responses to the alarm clock were different, but neither understood the full implications for their intimacy of this difference. At one point it had seemed very minor; after all, what difference does it make how you feel at five o'clock in the morning? But it turns out to make a great deal of difference, as do all kinds of other small things when they are assembled into a system in which two people brush up against the rough edges of each other's personalities.

Perceive the situation for this young couple. One has to presume they are young, because an older couple would have long since worked out some sort of adjustment. The time before breakfast is for the man the time when he would most like to make love, and for the wife it is the time she would least like to make love or do anything else either. His hungers imperiously demand union, and her early morning grogginess demands with equal imperiousness that she be left alone. The husbands begins to feel that he is being treated like a rapist, and the wife begins to feel used with insensitivity and crudeness.

There are three things that could happen. The husband could accept being repulsed and decide that the early morning hours are "off limits," that it's too much trouble and not worth the resentment involved. But this does not mean that his desires will go away or that his frustrations will cease. It means that he will resent his wife's prebreakfast frigidity, and this resentment will contribute to a network of resentments which will inevitably exist in any relationship. He will lie there feeling cheated. The filmy nightgown, which should be an invitation, is at this time of the day a mocking barrier.

The woman could give in, as many women do. Yielding to her husband is part of her marital responsibility. If he wants her at such an absurd and idiotic hour, she has no choice but to go along with him; but he is crude and uncivilized, and she makes it quite clear to him that early morning lovemaking is a responsibility and not a pleasure. She doesn't get anything out of it, and she will give him as little as possible.

Or the couple can fight. In the conflict they will reveal to each other for the first time what five o'clock in the morning really means to them. The husband will begin to understand what it is like to wake up every morning with a hangover, even if one had nothing to drink the night before. The wife will begin to understand—perhaps with envy—the sanguine serenity of the person who passes from sleep to full consciousness in a fraction of a second. In this exchange of understanding, the two young people will realize that each erred in his interpretation of the other's behavior and learn the real reason for that behavior. What looked like the absence of love or inconsiderateness or insensitivity was really a very simple—though fundamental—biological difference. They are now able to laugh at their differences and work out some kind of balance or compromise. What it will be is something only they can decide, but the important point is that the compromise would have been impossible had it not been for the clarification that emerged from the self-revelation occasioned by conflict.

Not all conflict, of course, ends so happily. (And this one may not either. Those biological differences will persist and compromises will have to be made and remade.) One can take it as axiomatic that the longer the conflict is put off, the more likely it is that the pain, anger, and resentment will blind lovers to the self-revelation in a conflict situation. Their fight will not be an attempt to communicate and understand, to clarify and resolve, so much as an attempt to hurt and punish. The critical point in the conflict, of course, is the laughter, for laughter is a turning point when passionate anger is transformed into passionate love. Laughter occurs at the moment when self-revelation is effectively communicated. The two lovers say in effect, "Oh, that's what you mean!" And however violent the fight may have been, effective self-revelation reveals that the issue is relatively minor. Any difference is relatively minor when compared to the fear that love no longer exists. The conflict ritual permits the two lovers to assert their fear that there is no love, to discover that the cause of tension is much less important, laugh at its relative triviality, and then take steps to eliminate it if possible or at least to integrate it into their lives.

The wife in our parable will never be as wide awake as her husband in the early morning, and he will never be as groggy as she at that time; but they can come to understand each other's responses and to realize that they do not call into question their basic love for each other. They will both have to adjust; they will both have to modify their behavior; they will both have to act against powerful physical feelings on occasion. But neither will demand of the other that they stop being what they are.

The husband will decide that early morning sex, however delightful, is something that will not occur as frequently as he would like. It will happen sometimes, but, all things considered, it would be better for him to seek other times for prime sexual activity.

The wife, on the other hand, will comprehend that for a man whose physiology is like that of her husband, love before breakfast is important and meaningful. At least some of the time, his desire for early morning sex is reasonable. She knows now that having understood their different responses to the alarm clock, he will want to make love at that hour only when his sexual hungers are extremely strong, and when he feels that way about her, she will be not only willing to respond but eager to do so even if the world and her head are both dull, leaden masses. More than that, since she is a smart woman, she will occasionally pick a morning and set out to seduce her husband when he least expects it. She knows that if he goes to work with an experience like that fresh in his mind, he will be only too eager to get home in the evening. A time of such obvious sexual vulnerability in her husband is simply too good an opportunity for a wife who is both clever and loving to pass up.

The example is both comic and elementary. Comic because the mismatch of the physiology of sleeping and waking in the couple is ludicrous. It is one of God's little jokes that at first is not very funny, but once they have faced it and resolved it, it becomes as hilarious to them as it apparently was to God. It is elementary because the differences between the man and woman are simply physiological; they are not (at least necessarily) connected with personality differences rooted in their childhood experiences. The conflict is not an easy one to solve. No conflict in intimacy is easy to solve, but it is much easier to resolve than other more complicated ones. The pattern of possible solutions is always the same. Either the husband or the wife gives in or they have a fight in which they reveal the reasons for the tension and move toward resolution.

What is important in the marriage is that the couple develop a style and a ritual in which conflict can be waged as often as is necessary without threatening the structure of the marriage. However difficult it may be to develop ritualized ways of dealing with conflict, such rituals are still necessary. A classic example of ritualized conflict in American society is the collective bargaining situation. Management and labor need each other in the economic sphere as much as the husband and wife do in the domestic sphere. Tensions build up between them in the course of a contract. The renegotiation period is a time of tension release, of angry threats, loud warnings, harsh and bitter words. Despite the rhetoric and an occasional well-publicized strike, most contracts are renegotiated successfully and management and labor settle down to another several years of peaceful cooperation. The rituals are not unimportant. They provide for a release of anger, they clarify the situation, they make needs and problems explicit; but both sides know that the fundamental relationship between the union and the company is much too important for both of them to call it into ultimate question. Even if there was a strike, both sides know that it will be settled.

A ritual for conflict, then, must be developed in any relationship. The ritual does not mean that the conflict is not real; it means that the two partners have evolved a mechanism for dealing with tension that allows them to simultaneously express their anger and indicate to each other that the fundamental relationship is not in jeopardy. The style depends on the people involved. The ritual for some people seems to involve constant bickering, which in other couples would surely indicate that the marriage was in deep trouble, but for them it is a means of communicating with each other that reinforces the marriage union rather than threatens it. In other families conflict ritual involves much shouting and violent language. (I have been led to believe by some of my colleagues that in Jewish families this is the most appropriate and desirable—and enjoyable form of family conflict.) In other relationships the rhetoric of conflict and conflict resolution is much milder. On the whole it seems to me (and here I may be betraying my Irish familial background) that peace is better than shouting, but shouting is infinitely better than silence, and at times may be absolutely essential.

Conflict in intimate relationships ought not to be limited to pyrotechnic interludes. It should be an ongoing part of the relationship. Lovers must confront each other constantly in the process of self-revelation and self-disclosure. Most of the time, confrontation goes on at a low key. The ritual of conflict in the relationship has been so arranged that minor problems and tensions can be handled almost automatically and implicitly. When a problem is minor and when it is major, when it can be solved in the routine of day-to-day confrontation and when it requires a slam-bang mammoth confrontation depends upon the people involved and their progress in emitting and receiving recognizable cues. Like everything else in intimacy, skill in resolving conflict is only incompletely learned and only imperfectly exercised. Like every other skill, the lovers must always strive to improve their skills at conflict.

In some of the oversimplified versions of group dynamics theory that are currently being practiced, the word "confrontation" has come to mean brutal, vicious, thoughtless attacks on other people. The confrontations so applauded by the sensitivity cults are absolutely disastrous for any relationship, especially for an intimate one. There must be skill and tact and tenderness in every confrontation between lovers.

But it does not follow that in confrontation one pulls punches. If confrontation is to be tactful and tender, it also must be direct, sincere, and to the point. Sometimes I think the appeal of the overkill of the sensitivity cults is that it provides an escape from the much more complicated task of combining directness and tenderness in the confrontation situation.

A confrontation is a demand for the best in the other. It says in effect, "I chose you for a spouse (or a friend) because I saw in you certain admirable qualities. I will not settle for anything less than those qualities. You are a person who is capable of excellence, and it is excellence that I want and nothing else."

The need for confrontation is most obvious in the genital relationship. I knew once of a woman—obviously and clearly frustrated in the early years of her marriage—who presented her husband with a book on sexual techniques as a hint that he had quite a bit to learn about how to sexually satisfy her. He resolutely refused to look at it. Obviously, she should have been much more direct and blunt. She should have told him in no uncertain terms that she needed much more from him. She had chosen him as a husband, after all, because she believed that he had the strong masculine capacity to bring her to the fullness of sexual pleasure. He was not doing this. He was cheating her—however unintentionally—probably because he was afraid to experiment, afraid to risk himself in sex play that he feared she might reject. He needed to be encouraged to become much more demanding and challenging on the marriage bed, but he would not be so encouraged unless it was clear that not only did she want him to do so but that she absolutely demanded that he begin to enjoy her body and to bring enjoyment to it in a far more elaborate way than he had done thus far. I fear that merely giving him a book to read was something less than the vigorous confrontation that the two of them needed.

In another and exactly opposite situation, a husband had married a woman who was certainly not frigid but she "didn't get much out of sex." As her husband complained, "She always closes her eyes when we are making love." It was time for him to make it perfectly clear to her that he married her, at least in part, because he wanted her body—all of it, not just the minor part of it that was offered to him in their unsatisfactory lovemaking. He would simply not tolerate her foolish anxieties and scruples. I am afraid, however, that his tactics were just the opposite. If she wasn't getting much out of sex, then it didn't seem appropriate that he should get much out of it either, and so the two of them sought satisfaction in other aspects of their relationship and pretended that what went on in bed at night was not all that important.

Both these stories are so typical as to be normal. Sexual adjustment in both couples was poor because there was no effective communication about sexual needs, desires, problems, and fears. In neither case did the husband have any clear confidence in his ability to arouse his wife and hence hadn't even really tried. In both cases, the wife who desperately wanted to be aroused was incapable of bluntly telling her husband that his techniques in lovemaking were not up to his obvious masculine strengths. As a result, there was no satisfaction, no confrontation, no resolution, and, increasingly, no sex.

Confrontation is demanding what is wanted and what there is a right to. The young husband whose wife keeps her eyes shut during lovemaking has a right to something more. He married her in part because he thought that she would writhe in joy when he united his body with hers and thereby give unmistakable confirmation to his powers as a man. He has a right to such confirmation and ought to directly and vigorously demand it. In no uncertain terms he should tell his wife that he will settle for nothing less and that her shame and prudery are intolerable.

Similarly, the young wife who is getting no satisfaction out of intercourse should not be content with the gift of a book to her husband. She has a right to sexual satisfaction and she should demand that right. In the clearest possible terms she should tell her husband that so far he has been a failure as a lover and that she expects far more skillful passion from him—immediately. It is time that he begin to use her body the way it was intended to be used.

Unfortunately for the man in the one marriage and the woman in the other, "making demands" runs against what they have been taught that love is. In their family lives, they have learned that love means putting up with and going along with frustration and disappointment. One demonstrates love by being tolerant and not making demands. Love, in other words, means martyrdom, giving up one's own desires in order not to displease the other.

They have been taught what is not true. In fact, a love that is not passionate enough to demand the best from the other is not love at all.

But if the need for confrontation, conflict, and communication is especially obvious in the genital dimensions of a human relationship, it is in a way more simple when the subject is lovemaking. One is, after all, dealing with behavior that is relatively uncomplicated and with techniques that are relatively well known, at least in fantasy. Most men in their fantasy lives know exactly how to arouse their wives, but they are afraid to risk converting their fantasy into reality. Virtually every woman knows quite clearly and quite explicitly what it takes to make her husband feel supremely and ecstatically masculine, yet she is afraid to act on her knowledge in fear that her own defenses will be shattered permanently by such behavior. Communication and resolution are relatively easy where the problem is the need for progress in sexual adjustment. To say that the challenge is "relatively easy" is not to say that all that many people respond to it. It is simply to assert that the other problems of human intimacy are both more complex to describe and more difficult to resolve. There is both a fantasy and a folklore which men and women can fall back upon in providing sexual satisfaction for themselves and each other; there is much less folklore and almost no fantasy about how we adjust to intimacy with the person who is different from us—different not only in body but in personality. It is very unlikely that in marriage psychological conflicts can be worked out unless some basically satisfying modality of sexual adjustment has been achieved. If a husband and wife do not have fun with each other in bed, they will have neither the motivation nor the courage to tackle the more complex problems in a personality conflict. But being honest and blunt with each other about what is required for satisfactory intercourse is only the beginning—though a necessary one —for working out the ritual of conflict in the marriage.

Confrontation is not something distinct from the rhythm of taking and being taken in any human friendship. It is not a diversion from the process but a continuation and a furtherance of it. It can only occur when two people are confident enough of themselves and of their relationship to know that it can survive conflict and occasional acts of confrontation. But if this minimum confidence in the relationship does not exist and if conflict and confrontation cannot occur, then the two people who pretend to intimacy may continue to exist in some sort of physical or psychological juxtaposition, but friends and lovers they are not.

9
Loneliness

There are two kinds of loneliness that afflict human life. The first is the loneliness that comes from the human condition. It can be mitigated and alleviated but it cannot be eliminated. The other is the loneliness that we choose freely. It can always be conquered if we choose to do so.

We are, for weal or woe, consciously individuated creatures. No love, however permanent or however powerful, makes us more than finite. We may occasionally break through the boundaries of our finitude in moments of ecstasy. But these moments experienced in mystic contemplation or at the height of sexual arousal are fleeting, and we find ourselves all too quickly alone again, cut off, isolated. Genital love even at its most rewarding does not eliminate finitude though it can be a powerful motivation for temporarily achieving union. It alleviates, however transiently, the pain and isolation of finitude, and that is all that can be asked of it. Even the most ecstatic of experiences still leaves one lonely because it still leaves one finite. It is in these experiences that man feels most poignantly his hunger for the infinite. That there is an Infinite, incidentally, does not seem a matter for doubt during or immediately after moments of ecstasy. Such confidence in the Infinite is not,

I think, exactly a "proof" that there is a Lover "out there" who will be able to end our loneliness. It rather reassures us of the existence of that love. It may well be the most important reassurance.

In addition to such existential loneliness, there is also the loneliness we freely choose. Even if man may not break completely with his finitude and isolation, his life is filled with opportunities to move beyond the barriers of individuation to find psychological and physical union with others. The pleasures and delights of life and love are obvious and demanding. Our bodies and our spirits are designed to seek union with others, but the design does not deprive us of our freedom. We can turn away from others; we can permit ourselves to be permanently rebuffed by them; we can lose our nerve, our courage, our imagination, our capacity for surprise. We can settle for a dull, monotonous, isolated, drab existence. We can do these things despite the primal thrust for union of body and spirit which is at the core of our personalities. To some extent, all of us choose this path of loneliness. One's giving and taking is always imperfect and inadequate. We are distracted, worried, anxious; and love is a very incomplete effort. What is important, however, is not perfection but persistence—a continuation of efforts to succumb to desire, to break out of fears, to become vigorous, challenging, surprising lovers. Even if their efforts seem to involve loss of dignity and propriety and leave them open to ridicule, lovers must persist.

Our existential loneliness is part of the human condition. Any celibate who thinks that if he had a spouse his life would have meaning and purpose and that he would be able to escape the finitude and imperfection that plagues him is naive about both sexuality and meaning. How we interpret sexual experience is not at all dictated by the experiences themselves. Nor does sexuality remove the pains of isolation and individuation for very long. It does provide us with powerful motives and powerful rewards for not surrendering to isolation and withdrawing permanently behind the impenetrable barriers of loneliness. But a man whose life has no meaning before he finds a mate, who is mired down in his own distrust and suspicion, will find neither purpose nor cure for his loneliness amid the delights a woman's body offers. She is made to be enjoyed (as, indeed, a man is made to be enjoyed), but joy does not give faith and it does not heal fear. It may give a greater reason for faith and a more powerful drive against fear, but by itself pleasure is no cure for the sickness of spirit.

What sexuality does make possible—and in this respect the sexuality need not be genital—is affection and tenderness. And perhaps in the final analysis this is what women and men most need and most want in their lives. Orgasms are nice, but affection and tenderness are indispensable. A lover does indeed provide delight, but he also protects, provides care, and helps to avoid discouragement, weariness, and boredom. No lover can eliminate these things from his (or her) life unless he (or she) is willing to fight them; but in moments when the fight seems scarcely worth the effort, the lover can show that it is. It is precisely in these moments that human love is most rewarding, most pleasurable, and most important. Whoever loves and whatever be the nature of this love, if the lover knows when to say the kind word and to apply the gentle touch, when to laugh and smile, when to encourage and to show solicitude, when to sympathize with frustrations and to ridicule hesitancies, then the lover has immense power.

The need for affection of this kind is specifically human. It occurs only in creatures capable of reflection and who have devised symbols that give meaning to their behavior. But because affection is uniquely human, it becomes the indispensable prerequisite for human love. No matter how skilled the eroticism or genitality of lovers may be, if they do not make love in an atmosphere permeated by affection and tenderness, then their love will not be humanly satisfying. Man wants pleasure, of course, but he wants with it reassurance and comfort, and if these qualities are absent the pleasure really isn't all that much fun. The most delightful lovemaking among married couples is precisely that which is explicitly designed to alleviate loneliness, discouragement, and weariness. It is then that love most effectively communicates to the other that he is worth something, that he is desired, admired, and loved. The wife comes to distract her husband from the worries of his work with herself and the martini pitcher. She is saying that however serious the work problems may be and however much he may be discouraged, it has nothing to do with his own goodness and desirability. She loves him and wants him no matter what happens, and she is willing to engage in "shameless" behavior to make it as clear as possible to him how much she wants him and how important he is to her no matter what else happens.

And a husband who gently calms his wife at the end of what was for her a nerve-racking, compulsive, and distracting day is telling her in effect that even if she feels she has failed to meet all of the multitudinous responsibilities that she could have coped with in the course of the day, she is still his and the source of constant delight to him not because of what she accomplished today but because of who she is. As the nightgown slips from her body, she knows not merely that she can give pleasure but also that she is a person who is cared for. That makes both the pleasure she gives and receives more intense.

Perhaps the reason for much of the infidelity that occurs in the early middle years of life is precisely that tenderness and affection have gone out of the marriage. It has become a series of obligations and responsibilities. Career (for one or for both), children, social life, political involvement, intellectual concerns—all of these use up time and energy, and while the two people still have intercourse with each other, it becomes more of a mechanical ritual than an act of reassurance and affection.

It is at just such times that a person most obviously needs affection and is most likely to attract it from others. Similarly, at such times affection offered or even available can become irresistible. One gets into an affair not so much for genital release (though that is surely to be had), not so much for erotic excitement (though that is certainly present), but so that one might experience a few moments of tenderness and reassurance. One may even know that such reassurance and affection is transient, shallow, and deceptive. Nonetheless, in times of loneliness and discouragement even shallow reassurance and transient affection will be eagerly accepted when nothing else is available.

In other instances, husband and wife withhold affection from each other not because they are thoughtless or distracted but because they deliberately intend to punish each other. The inevitable conflict between them is not faced but repressed; desire is converted into anger and delight into vindictiveness. All the slights, the insensitivities, the disappointments, and the frustrations build up and affection is refused precisely at the times when it is most obviously needed. Heaven help the other person if in desperation he turns to someone else for affection, because that provides even more grounds for punishment.

The vindictive withholding of affection (and one can concede one's body without offering affection) is one of the most ugly things a man or a woman can do. In the strict sense of the word, it is hateful. In the old days, Catholic women used to feel constrained to confess when they had refused their "marital duty." What they meant, of course, was that they had refused to have intercourse with their husbands, but the "marital duty," or indeed the duty of any love, goes far beyond physical union. What really ought to be confessed before God and men is the refusal to offer tenderness, affection, reassurance, and comfort to our lover at times when he or she most clearly needs it. There are times, of course, when people can be excused for not having intercourse, but there are no times, so long as there is anything left of the relationship, when they can be excused from tenderness and comfort.

It is man's loneliness and his need for affection that make possible those two difficult and pleasurable experiences between lovers, reconciliation and new beginnings. Not all conflict can be routinized; not all problems can be resolved. Confrontation may lead to a breakdown in the relationship, and fear may so impede communication that lovers become strangers. To begin again means to admit one's past mistakes, accept responsibility for one's failures, write off all the wasted time, and go back, as it were, to ground zero to begin again. Such a wiping clean of the slate, which involves both forgiving the other and oneself, is not an easy task. A married couple in their late thirties or early forties will be greatly humiliated to admit to each other that their genital life is dull and always has been. It will be tough for the man to concede that he has been inept and clumsy in his attempts to give pleasure to his wife. It will be hard for her to admit that part of the reason for his clumsiness has been her silence and another part of it has been that she long since gave up trying to be seductive. They must go back to the beginning and pretend that they are newlyweds, or, perhaps more appropriately, that they are engaged in an illicit love affair. Indeed, by the standards of the routine to which their life together has sunk, any change will look like an illicit love affair. Each new beginning will not be easy, for it will mean that two people have learned from the mistakes that occurred in their relationship without holding these mistakes against each other. There are delights in reconciliation, of course, and a love affair which begins for the first time or anew at forty can be infinitely more pleasurable than one that begins at eighteen, for both lovers have much more experience, both physical and psychological, to bring to their affair. The past can be an asset as well as a liability, particularly if the lovers are able to develop a capacity to laugh at the grotesqueries of their past mistakes. They had better be able to laugh, because that is the only thing that will exorcise the anger and the humiliation of those mistakes.

It is the need for affection and reassurance that is the most powerful motivation for beginning anew. Most lovers cannot or will not end their relationship unless it has become completely intolerable. There are too many things at stake. It is much better to stumble along in an unsatisfactory relationship than risk the public conflict, complication, and disgrace that would come from ending it. While extramarital interludes may provide temporary affection and reassurance, they tend to become unsatisfactory in the long run. One will find comfort and affection with one's spouse or probably not at all. Of course, there is a strong strain toward renewing affection because the couple have been lovers before, and are still, to some greater or lesser extent.

What has happened is that love and hatred have been powerfully intermixed in their relationship. The ambivalence that is involved in every intimacy is now both a serious problem and a last opportunity. The man and woman really do not like each other very much and have stored up all sorts of resentments. On the other hand, there are strong ties that unite them, and they can on occasion provide each other with both reassurance and pleasure.

In most marriages that have grown cool if not cold, there is in both people a latent desire to begin again, though, unfortunately, they have grown skilled in ignoring the cues that the other emits about the possibility of starting anew. What is required to begin a reconciliation is that when one person sees a tentative sign of affection and reassurance from the other, he or she should quickly respond with similar affection. There is, of course, considerable risk in either offering or responding to affection offered in a relationship that has become routine if not cool. In a way, it is an even bigger risk than beginning a love relationship, for now one knows all the things that can go wrong, and one also knows that if one attempts to renew a relationship and the other turns him down, it will make matters worse instead of better. Unfortunately, offers for renewal are frequently turned down. No one suspects that if such offers are firm enough, persistent enough, and imaginative enough, they will ultimately become irresistible in most cases.

A reconciliation involves winning a husband or wife all over again. It can be an exhilarating, fascinating, fun-filled experience. Indeed, any good marriage is a never-ending series of reconciliations. The more frequent the minor ones, the less need there will be to go through the pain of having a love relationship hit rock bottom before it begins to be reborn.

It frequently seems to those who are presented with an opportunity to begin again, to rebuild a relationship, that they are being asked to do something heroic and extraordinary. Winning each other all over again in the middle years of life seems ludicrous and absurd and simply not the thing to do. If, despite the evidence of realistic common sense, two people do begin anew, each of them may feel that what they are doing ought to be greatly rewarded. In a way they are correct. What they are doing is heroic and the rewards may very well be great, but any other course is the sheerest sort of folly. One either seeks reconciliation or settles down to a life of drab, affectionless routine in which there is no excitement, no tenderness, no affection, no reassurance. Our whole existence ought to be a constant refusal of such an alternative. No matter how much humiliation and forgiveness are involved, we must not choose loneliness.

10

Fidelity and Sexuality

Fidelity is part of every human friendship. It is the strain toward permanence and toward public commitment to permanence that is involved in any relationship beyond the most superficial. Fidelity is a longing for love that does not end.

Since every human relationship except the most transient has a sexual component to it, one can say that sexual fidelity ought to be a characteristic of all meaningful human relationships. The style of fidelity may vary from rerelationship to relationship. A man is faithful to another man who is his friend in a very different way than he is faithful to his wife. Similarly, he may be faithful to a woman who is a close friend in a very different way from the fidelity he exercises toward his wife. In this chapter we shall speak of fidelity between lovers who are permanently committed to one another with a special emphasis on genital fidelity. It should be clear that, as in so many other things, genital fidelity is merely a model and a symbol of a much more general aspect of human relationships.

The promise to be faithful to one's friend is by its very nature both permanent and public. A faithfulness that is secret is a peculiar kind of faithfulness, indeed, because as long as it is secret one has the much easier option of going back on it. A man or a woman who intends to be faithful is eager to announce this fidelity to the whole community and to have the community ratify it. Faithfulness by its very nature seeks the public domain. Nor does faithfulness have any restrictions, limitations, or qualifications. When one pledges fidelity to a friend, he doesn't do it on a tentative basis or for a limited period of time or subject to an option for later renewal. Fidelity that is not aimed toward permanence is not fidelity at all.

I do not think that there can be much serious question that both public ratification and permanence are part of the notion of fidelity no matter what sort of relationship that fidelity characterizes. Having made this observation, let me note that the purpose of this chapter is not to make any judgment about such circumstances that might arise in a marriage when it might be concluded either that the promise of fidelity was never truly meant or that, for one reason or another, it may now no longer be considered binding. Neither do I propose to address myself to the question of whether a public and permanent commitment to another person may occur before it is solemnly ratified in a marriage ceremony. Hence, I will not speak of the question of divorce or the possibility of premarital sex. I refuse to address myself to these questions because they are beyond the scope of this book and because I think they can be addressed intelligently only after the material presented in this chapter is reflected upon.

It is interesting that the almost universally accepted definition of marital fidelity focuses on whether one engages in sexual activity outside of marriage. The faithful person is one who does not have intercourse outside of marriage. In no other context is fidelity defined in such narrow and negative terms. Indeed, normally the word conveys a highly positive connotation; but in marriage, fidelity merely means that one doesn't do certain things. It is at least possible that such a narrow and negative definition of marital fidelity has become widespread because it is much more difficult to follow the positive implications of the concept of fidelity in marriage than it is to stay out of someone else's bed.

Fidelity in any relationship is a permanent commitment to "reach out" for the other, a promise to persist in efforts to transcend the barriers and the distance that separate one from the other, a firm resolve to maintain effort in sustaining and developing the relationship no matter what difficulties and trials arise.

Genital fidelity, then, means that one is firmly committed to developing, enriching, and expanding the genital relationship with one's partner no matter how many frustrations, disappointments, and failures may intervene. The faithful lover is committed to developing his own skills, sensitivities, and capacities as a sexual being, particularly by learning through the "feedback" he receives from the other's response to him. He promises to give himself over to the physical and verbal dialogue which is required if his hesitant and tentative physical resources are to become firm, confident, and effective.

The faithful lover, then, engages in ongoing effort to improve the seductiveness of his erotic self-display. He constantly seeks to improve and refine his skills at bringing pleasure to the other. He develops his capacity for tenderness and especially his skill at combining tenderness with arousal. He arouses his partner in such a way that the weariness, discouragement, weakness, and fear which beset her or him are assuaged precisely in the process of responding to his (or her) sexual advances.

Simultaneously, he strives ever more effectively to open up his own inner self, with all its fragility, vulnerability, and weaknesses, to the other so that the other may perceive his need for tenderness, affection, and gentleness, particularly when those qualities are communicated by the caress, the kiss, an embrace, a touch, a contact between warm and aroused bodies.

No one, be it noted, is born with such refined skills. While fantasy lives give general outlines, they do not provide detailed sets of instructions. The skills and sensitivities and capacities of being effective bed partners come only through practice, trial and error, through the ability to laugh at blunders, and, of course, from getting feedback from a partner. If a lover cannot persuade the one with whom he couples on the marriage bed to tell him what he is doing right and what wrong, then improvement is most unlikely. Fidelity means, then, that a lover asks for, indeed demands such feedback; that it is done in such a way that the instructions from the other, be they in word or action, are a pleasure to give.

For a man to persist in this kind of fidelity is much more difficult than to turn away from the curvacious body of a woman other than his wife when that body signals its availability to him. Rejecting the offer of a new body requires courage and strength of rather limited duration. Trying to improve one's capacity to bring pleasure to and obtain pleasure from a body which is next to one in bed every night is a challenge that never ends.

Similarly, a woman may have to push her resources to the limit to turn away from caresses that seem to almost set her on fire; but once she has turned away, she is not likely to have to turn away again from those hands if she has been definite in her rejection. The crisis was fierce but passing. Her husband's hands, however, are always present, capable indeed of bringing her great pleasure even though at times they may be clumsy and inept and occasionally totally lacking in attractiveness. Her commitment is not merely to permit her husband's hands to roam about her body but to guide them, help them, make them stronger and more confident. That is not a challenge of half an hour; it is the challenge of a lifetime.

Fidelity also means a commitment to increasing sensitivity to the other. First of all, the faithful lover has pledged himself to becoming ever more sophisticated in his understanding of the physiology of his genital partner. A man may know about women's physiology in general and still know nothing of his wife's. And unless fidelity means for him the responsibility of tenderly and gently exploring her body and her responses to that exploration, he will never know. That a very considerable number of men have only the most remote notions of the physiological responses of women and practically no notion at all of the particular responses of their wives indicates how little this dictate of fidelity is honored.

In our culture it is assumed that a man's physiological response is more obvious than a woman's. Hence, a wife may feel that she does indeed understand the physiology of her husband and there is no further need to explore his body. What he is looking for is obvious enough, and there is no need for subtlety or nuance or delicacy in what she does. But in fact the flesh and the nervous system of a man are as delicate and responsive as they are in a woman. There are an infinite variety of shadings and nuances in what a woman can do to the body of a man. When either partner thinks there is nothing more to be learned, then the commitment to growth and self-transcendence in a genital relationship is in trouble.

But fidelity also implies the desire to grow in understanding of the psycho-sexual needs and dispositions of the partner. The one who is loved is more than a collection of sexual organs, primary and secondary, to be stimulated. He or she also possesses a rich, complex fantasy life, and the lover wishes to penetrate into this fantasy life because the lover seeks more knowledge and because the fantasy life is the raw material for maintaining surprise and wonder in lovemaking.

The faithful lover learns how to read the defense mechanisms of his genital partner with skills like that with which the professional quarterback reads the defensive secondary. For, just as in football, the defenses change as the circumstances change, so in lovemaking the moods, the fears, the hopes, the frustrations of a given situation may make for a rather different set of defense mechanisms than the ones which existed last night or may exist tomorrow night. Similarly, the faithful lover does all in his power to increase his sensitivity to the cues that his beloved emits, indicating the need for tenderness and affection. He works hard to learn how to overcome the other's reluctance to talk about what happens when the last garment is laid aside and the erectile tissues begin to prepare for union.

Finally, the faithful lover strives to become gracious in the techniques of providing the other with the needed feedback in such a way as to enhance rather than weaken fundamental self-esteem as a sexual person and as a genital partner. To inform, instruct, correct, lead in a way that enhances self-esteem is no easy task. It requires delicacy, tact, discretion, and also the ability to ultimately say exactly what one means. No one knows naturally how to communicate with others in such a fashion, particularly when the subject is as sensitive and primordial as lovemaking; and, yet, unless man and woman are committed to growing in such skills and helping each other to grow, it is not clear that their marriage ought to be described as a faithful one.

The use I have made of the notion of fidelity in this chapter seems strange only because we have been willing to accept a narrow, negative definition of the term. I am arguing that fidelity means only in a secondary and relatively unimportant way that we do not commit adultery. In a primary and positive way it means that married lovers are committed to developing a pleasurable genital relationship that has within it the capacity for ever more development no matter how many obstacles or difficulties or frustrations or disappointments may be encountered. One might add that fidelity seems almost necessarily to involve a commitment on the part of lovers that they will never stop laughing at their mistakes, ineptitudes, and blunders; for if they cannot sustain their capacity for laughter, it is to be feared that laughter's cynical surrogate, ridicule, will intervene. Laughter can unite lovers psychologically, first, and then physically; ridicule divides, separates, and isolates.

What has been described in this chapter is merely genital fidelity: the commitment to increasing both one's own pleasure and the pleasure of the spouse. Of course, genital fidelity is only part of the more total human fidelity that should permeate the whole marriage relationship. However critical a symbol it may be of the marriage relationship, it is subsidiary to the wider meaning of fidelity in marriage, as in any friendship. Fidelity in this broader sense means the permanent, public, solemn, and irrevocable commitment to dedicate one's life to bringing out the best in both one's partner and oneself. It is most unlikely that a man and woman will be able to do this unless there is a strong commitment to increasing the amount of enjoyment that occurs in sexual relations. On the other hand, if there is not a relationship in which two people are committed to a whole life of challenging the best that is in each other, then it is not likely that the union of sex organs will continue to be very enjoyable.

It is interesting to observe that many married people experience great feelings of guilt when they sleep with someone else but relatively little feeling of guilt when they allow the nightly or thrice weekly romp on the marriage bed to become dull and routine. The husband will torment himself about a transient affair with a woman at work or a brief fling when he is away at a convention. These are acts of infidelity, but it will never occur to him that a continuing infidelity occurs when he acquiesces in the static and stagnant genital relationship with his wife.

Similarly, a woman will torment herself (and frequently her confessor) endlessly about an episode of infidelity when she seduces or permits herself to be seduced by the handsome, virile man across the street one day when his wife and her husband were away somewhere else. She will not permit herself even the slightest consideration of the possibility that there may have been mitigating circumstances, and she would be horrified at the suggestion that a basic infidelity permeates the whole relationship with her husband because she has permitted it to become dissatisfying and uninteresting. The human race continues to strain at the gnat and swallow the camel.

Fidelity, then, means a refusal to give up on a relationship. Genital fidelity means the refusal to give up on the possibility of enhancing the excitements and the satisfactions available in the union between a male and a female body. Marital fidelity, in the most general sense, means that a husband and wife refuse to give up on their relationship until every last possible effort has been expended.

Infidelity is not the same thing as adultery, at least in its primary meaning. Infidelity means quitting, giving up on any aspect of a relationship when there are still possibilities remaining. Adultery frequently may be the result of this primordial infidelity, and it may also contribute to an infidelity that is spreading through a relationship like a cancer; but as long as there is a commitment to continue efforts to try to expand and to grow, to be a better, more generous, and more effective lover, then adultery does not

of itself destroy the primary fidelity of a genital relationship. It is an unfortunate and ugly incident, but it does not
necessarily revoke a primary commitment.

Fidelity assumes that the basic evaluation of the other,
which led to the original commitment, was a correct one; it
may have been naive or incomplete, but it was a commitment which saw something valuable and admirable in the
other. The other was initially perceived as fun to be with,
fun to look at in the nude, challenging to go to bed with,
and exciting enough to want to spend a lifetime with. The
frustrations, disappointments and disillusionments that
have intervened since that initial commitment cannot help
but call it into question. Fidelity persists in believing that
the original valuation was correct and that it would be a
mistake to abandon without further effort the struggle to
achieve the good things that the original commitment
promised.

Essential to fidelity is gentleness. We are all of us fragile,
uncertain, vulnerable, insecure, hesitant people. The more
we act as though we are not, the more we reveal our own
weakness. Only the strong person can admit that he is
weak. There are few human relationships and few marriages that will not notably improve when the gentleness
level in the relationship is increased.

If what happens in the marriage bed is not pervaded by
gentleness, it is likely to be both unsatisfying and infre-
quent. Sophisticated lovers know that in the bedroom or
anywhere else gentleness has incredible erotic power. A
kiss at the nape of the neck, a contact of two hands, an
arm around the waist, tentative pressure of a knee against
a thigh, fingers brushing lightly and quickly across a breast
—all of these gentle actions have much more powerful
erotic impact than do the acrobatics and gymnastics of the
sex manuals performed without gentleness. Fidelity, then,
is persistent, dauntless, implacable when needs be, chal-

lenging when challenge is called for, and, in the midst of everything, always gentle.

The most basic reason for lack of sexual satisfaction is neither cognitive nor psychological; it is rather existential. Many people lack the basic information, or at least the detailed information, to be adequate sexual partners. Many more—probably most—have psychological hangups that stand in the way of using the information they do have. Information can be obtained and psychological problems can be lessened by competent therapy. But unless they are willing to believe that they are lovable and attractive as human beings and that the risk of vulnerability is underwritten by a fundamentally gracious cosmos, their sex lives are not going to be especially rewarding.

A man may watch a full-color movie (of the sort currently being used in sex education) of a man bringing a woman to full climax with his hand. Such a movie may well impart potentially useful information and it will certainly arouse him erotically, but it will not persuade him that he is either a skillful lover or an attractive man unless his wife's attitude toward him leaves little doubt about it.

Similarly, a woman may digest all the suggestions of *The Sensuous Woman* and never consider using any of them in bed unless she is convinced that her husband loves her and finds her irresistible as a woman.

With few exceptions, lovers enter sexual relationships with very uncertain faith in their own attractiveness and competency. Those who behave most confidently are usually the most insecure. They need both the faith that they can take risks and the response of a lover whose desire is so apparent that it creates desirability. Neither information nor therapy—however useful and appropriate they may be—can in itself persuade one to take the risks of exposed vulnerability in a complete sexual relationship. Faith in the possibility of fidelity (as it has been described in this chapter) is essential if one is to go beyond information and therapy to the great adventure of sexual love.

Thus a spouse must face the fact that no matter how confident the other may seem, he (or she) is not really confident at all, and the absolutely essential prerequisite of sexual growth is to build up the other's confidence in his (or her) own sexuality. To the extent that one can persuade the partner that he (or she) is "good in bed"—or in any other dimension of the marriage—will the partner in fact become "good" there.

Fidelity means dedicating one's life to creating an irresistible lover out of a very human partner. The faithful man knows that unless his wife is convinced that it is her erotic appeal rather than his "needs" that turns him on whenever he is with her, she will not be much of a "playmate," and their marriage will be listless and dull. His conviction about her eroticism makes it possible for her to be erotic.

And the faithful woman knows that her husband will be clumsy and inept unless she conveys to him that she has no choice but to melt in his presence, that she desperately craves to feel his body inside of hers. Only then will he have enough confidence in his manhood to be the kind of man that can in fact send her into paroxysms of pleasure. In lovemaking you get what you earn.

Essential to creating an irresistible lover for oneself is knowing what to see. Every lover is physically capable of arousing a partner if only because the organs are meant to complement. Nor are there any partners so inept that there does not exist in them the faint stirrings of eroticism. They must then choose to "see" that which is attractive and erotic and ignore that which is still and awkward. If one chooses to invest the other with eroticism and gently helps to develop it, one has in fact yielded to the other's attractiveness. By selecting those aspects of behavior and person which can be developed into extreme eroticism, and by responding to such aspects, the lover makes it possible for them to be developed. By ignoring or brushing aside fears and hesitancies it is thus made possible for them to diminish. By selective perceptions a lover can make another what that partner is capable of becoming.

Of course, just the opposite can be done by choosing to ignore the first tentative movements of adult genitality and concentrating on the mistakes, the stiffness, the ridiculous false starts. Such a response drives the other back into his shell—freeing the one from the obligation to run the risks of growth.

And that is the essence of infidelity.

Part of the promise of fidelity, it seems to me, is the commitment to maintain physical attractiveness in keeping with one's age. Presumably, this means that the "overweight and out of shape" condition of most middle-class Americans is in some sense a violation of such a commitment. A man or a woman who permits the body to become flabby and fat is saying in effect that there is no need to maintain a sexually attractive appearance. There are two possible reasons for such a decision: either it is a means of keeping the lover at bay or it is a means of punishing oneself for sexual frustration and inadequacy. In either case, the body is being used as a barrier and not as a means of communication.

I will confess to being shocked at the number of young people still in their twenties who will pay large sums of money each year for clothes and cosmetics but are apparently willing to distort their bodies by eating too much and not exercising enough.

And the claim that being overweight has nothing to do with sexual fears and frustrations ought to be perceived as patently absurd in an era as informed on the teachings of Dr. Freud as ours claims to be.

In the entire range of the components of a marriage, what fidelity means is that one commits oneself never to wait for the other to take the initiative to heal a separation and never to reject the other's initiative no matter how awkward or inarticulate that initiative may be.

Fidelity means that when a woman wakes in the middle of the night from a frightening dream and feels lonely and worthless and afraid, she does not hesitate to reach for her husband, knowing that he has the strength, confidence, and tenderness to exorcise her primordial fears. It means that she knows not to seek his consolation under such circumstances would be infidelity, because it would mean that she is not willing to share with him her most intimate feelings of weakness.

Similarly, fidelity means that at the end of a frustrating, discouraging, humiliating day a husband knows that he can and must give the signals to his wife by which she will know that he needs an encounter with a primal, lifegiving earth mother who can smother his feelings of inadequacy with the delights of her flesh. Not to turn to her for comfort under such circumstances is also infidelity, because it means that he is not willing to share with her his most intimate weakness.

In every faithful relationship, there are turning points: decisive occasions when the whole tone and ambiance of the relationship is transformed. But there will be one point which is crucial because it points the way to all the others. Married couples whose genital interaction is satisfying emphasize that there was a time when their lovemaking went through a drastic transformation, when they were able simultaneously to shed their fears, their inhibitions, their uncertainties and confusions. Usually, such an event occurred when they found themselves saying and doing things that they never thought they could be able to say and do and couldn't quite believe in fact that they had taken the drastic risk that seemed to be involved. Once they crossed such a sexual Rubicon, everything that went before looked in retrospect like foolishness. Unfortunately, such decisive ventures into the land of sexual pleasure never happen in many marriages—though many times they *almost* happen. At the last moment, both man and woman lose their nerve.

A man may have many distractions and problems on his mind. He may have a whole host of critical responsibilities that must be thought about and acted upon; but when he senses that his wife is possessed by a feeling of worthlessness as a woman, he must mobilize all his resources as a man to convince her that she is wrong. Not a single sexually sensitive part of her body should remain untouched by his fiercely roaming fingers or lips. If he cannot restore her faith in her womanhood under such circumstances, he is worthless as a husband, no matter how many fur coats he may buy for her.

When a woman sees that her husband is battered and harried, discouraged and beaten, nothing is more important in her life than to comfort and caress him. His weary head must be pressed against her and her hands must blot out all the aches and pains of his existence. When she is finished loving him, life once again will be eminently worth living, if only because he knows that whatever else he may lose, she will always be there.

Such occasions of weakness and vulnerability are critically important in a marriage precisely because there are times when a lover has immense power over his (or her) mate. The power will be used either to break into a previously unexplored area of the other's selfhood to draw the lovers closer to one another, or it will be used to demolish an already bruised and fragile ego. It is a melancholy reflection on the state of contemporary American marriages to suspect that the latter is a much more frequent occurrence than the former.

But the faithful lover is constantly sensitive to the possibility that the other may be saying in word or deed, "Please, please love me *now*." For when that message is sent, the opportunity for growth in both physical love and personal pleasure is very great indeed. To miss such an opportunity is infidelity of the worst sort.

I take it that when fidelity is so understood, it is naturally an admirable characteristic. Despite the pseudo-sophistication of some of the sex literature, few people really admire infidelity. The playboy and the playmate may look attractive in the shallow glitter of Mr. Hefner's journal, but few would want to spend too much time with either of these characters. In fact, the whole appeal of the *Playboy* philosophy is that it promises quick pleasure without having to be involved with the rather dull pasteboard people who provide it. The ambiguity of fidelity consists in the fact that it is both admirable and difficult, both something to be valued highly and something that is very difficult to practice because it demands so much of our resources.

The struggle for fidelity—as that quality has been defined in this chapter—is difficult; but it is also pleasurable, indeed, immensely so. When two people are trying to grow in their mutual lovemaking, a psychological tone develops in their relationship that greatly enhances their attractiveness to each other. The fact of their joint effort is a partial guarantee of its success, precisely because the joy of their common quest makes them more pleasurable—both in the sense of being able to give and being able to receive pleasure—to one another. They love one another more because there is more to love.

Sleeping with someone else is always a radical possibility because they always have the physical capacity of coupling with anyone, but however powerful a transient inclination to do so may be, they are still likely to confine their genital activity to the marriage bed. With no other potential partner do they share the exquisite pain and the exquisite joy of the quest for fidelity. Other partners may *look* more attractive for a few moments or a few days, but the faithful lover knows that his (or her) permanent partner is more attractive because it took a long time to develop the acute sensitivity to the possibilities of pleasure that can be found in a faithful relationship. Familiarity breeds contempt only for those who have stopped growing. For faithful lovers, it breeds both heightened pleasure and even heightened mystery.

Can the Christian symbol system throw any light on the ambiguity of fidelity? Can it assure that this admirable but painful human characteristic is possible? It seems to me that these are the pertinent questions that we must ask. Whether premarital or extramarital sex is sinful is not nearly so important as whether Christianity can sustain the positive demands of faithfulness. If it can, then the question of sex outside of marriage can be answered within a religious context. If it cannot, then the church is simply one more ethical or moral lawgiver with nothing new or unique to add to human customs.

The reason why we Christians are faithful in our relationships to one another is that Yahweh is faithful to us. In that implacable assertion in the book of Exodus, "I am Yahweh your God," he made it perfectly clear that no matter what we did as his people, he would still be our God. And in the sexual imagery of Osee, Jeremiah, and Ezekiel, Yahweh emphasized that even though we whore with false gods, he will not seek another people. We might turn our backs on him; he will never turn his back on us. We might be unfaithful; he will never be unfaithful. The Good News that Jesus brought was in effect a renewal of that covenant. The cross and the resurrection were a new covenant precisely because they promised in a deeper and richer way Yahweh's fidelity. The Eucharist has frequently been compared to a wedding banquet precisely because it is a celebration of Yahweh's fidelity. to his bride, the church. Christians are faithful to one another in all their relationships because Yahweh's fidelity gives them the confidence that their own fidelity requires and because they understand that their fidelity is an exercise in their vocation of manifesting Yahweh's love to the world. When a Christian husband and wife are faithful to one another in the way I have described in this chapter, they are manifesting Yahweh's love to the world.

It is to be presumed that most married couples do not view the art of sexual intercourse as a reflection of Yahweh's fidelity, for after all it occurs in the privacy of their bedroom with the door closed and the lights dim. How could they possibly believe that improving their skills at bringing each other pleasure reflects God's implacable commitment to his people?

They don't think of these things, in all likelihood, because nobody has ever suggested to them that the quality of their love—of which sexual intercourse is, of course, at the very center—is the most effective way they have of revealing God's love to the rest of the world. To the extent that a man and woman have settled for a static and dull genital relationship, they have settled for a marriage which is a very inadequate reflection of God's love for mankind. And to the extent that they are committed to improving the surprise and pleasure, the excitement, the challenge of what goes on between the sheets, then they are reflecting God's commitment to his people.

It seems to me that this is the only fundamentally meaningful observation that Christianity can make on the subject of premarital or extramarital sex. We Christians are faithful to one another in all our relationships and especially in our marriages, because that is the way we reflect God's love for us. There may be social, psychological, philosophical, psychiatric, and legal arguments in favor of fidelity. I am not sure how effective these arguments are when the temptation to adultery is almost overwhelming. Perhaps the Christian perspective that I have sketched in this chapter is no more effective, but it seems to me that it is the one that is uniquely ours and the only one that we should spend much time emphasizing.

When I have made this argument, people have said to me, "Young people don't accept such an ideal." I am not sure how many young people would in fact reject the ideal of fidelity when it is described in the positive fashion I have attempted in this chapter, but if young people are so devoid of sensibility that they cannot appreciate the natural admirability of fidelity, then so much the worse for them, for they are dull and unperceptive. And if they do not believe that it is appropriate for Christians to reflect in their relationships the implacable fidelity of Yahweh to us, then, once again, so much the worse for them, because they are not Christians and they do not understand the wonder and joy of the Christian message.

My point is that we must begin with the fundamental Christian symbols if we are to make a unique contribution to the problem of human fidelity. If those to whom we are talking do not accept the Christian symbol system, if they are unwilling to believe in God's overwhelming fidelity toward us as manifested in his son Jesus, then religious dialogue between them and us is not possible. One does not begin the dialogue, in other words, by talking about premarital sex. Nor does one begin by talking about fidelity even in the positive sense I have used in this chapter. One begins by talking about God's fidelity to us and then by suggesting that such fidelity gives us both the strength and the motivation we need for the admirable but extraordinarily difficult human quality of faithfulness.

We have no reason to apologize for the ideal of Christian fidelity, be it the fidelity of a genital relationship or of any kind of human relationship. Fidelity is naturally admirable; the ideal of fidelity which reflects God's fidelity to us is religiously sensitive and inspiring. That many people will not accept the ideal does not mean that it is inadequate; it is not that it has, as G. K. Chesterton suggested in another context, "been tried and found wanting," but found hard and not tried.

If there is no reason to apologize for the ideal of Christian fidelity, there are plenty of reasons for apologizing for the narrow, negative, physiological definition that we have permitted to become identified with fidelity. It is time that we made it clear to all concerned that we will simply have no part in conversations that begin with "What's wrong, after all, with premarital intercourse?" From our point of view, the conversation should begin with "What's wrong with people who are not able to grow in pleasure and satisfaction, in giving and receiving in marital intercourse?"

11

Growth Through Death

Human sexuality is a burden, a burden as heavy as life itself. Conflict, loneliness, the need for wonder and surprise —all of these are part of the agony of the human condition. Humans can get much more satisfaction out of their sex lives than animals, but they have to work at it much harder. An animal does not need courage; he does not need to take risks; he merely does what his instincts tell him to do. Humans must have both courage and faith.

The young man whose passive wife closes her eyes when he is doing to her the things a man should be doing to a woman ought to be possessed by outraged fury. He ought to shake her angrily until her eyes open wide and shout, "Damn you! Look at me when I play with you!" Such a cry is as natural, as normal, and as inevitable as a cry of pain after one touches a hot stove. Those closed eyes and that limp, passive body give a devastating, if unintentional, rejection. And, yet, to give voice to that cry of anger requires bravery. It is perhaps easier, if frustrating, to accept her prudery and shame.

Similarly, the young woman whose husband is a timid and disappointing lover is scarcely being very effective when she buys him a book. She should face him with withering scorn and demand, "Don't you know anything about how to seduce a woman?" Again, the cry of anger and pain flows naturally from the depths of the woman's person, and it may humiliate and enrage her husband, but in these circumstances it will be curative. Drift, resentment, frustration require little courage; curative anger requires much.

The courage required for a demand of sexual response is great, but it covers only one situation, albeit a very important one. The courage to face the constant tensions, frictions, and conflict of a life of intimacy is even more difficult, because it is not a courage that demands great anger in one situation but rather great persistence in all situations. We can be very brave for short periods of time, but constant bravery is wearisome.

It also takes courage to emit those small cues and signals which say to the other, "Please care for me—now. I desperately need reassurance and affection." It takes equal courage to live a life that is always sensitive to the possibility that such cues are being emitted. Only the brave can permit others to see them as they really are. We are afraid to stand naked physically in the presence of another because we are so vulnerable stripped. We can be ridiculed, baited, hurt. We are even more afraid to be psychically vulnerable in the presence of the other. If he knows us as we really are, how can he help but share the disgust we feel for ourselves? About all one can say to a lover who is seeking the courage for physical and psychological self-revelation is that just as the other's body and person delight you rather than disgust you, so, incredible as it may seem, your body and your spirit are not only adequate to him but a source of constant fascination and joy. But the battle between courage and shame is an unending one, and the victories of courage are both difficult to wage and barely won.

We can say about love what was said of the military

history of Great Britain, that all battles were lost except
the last one. It doesn't matter whether courage triumphs
over shame by a slight margin; what matters is that it does
in fact triumph.

But something more is required to sustain wonder, courage, capacity for growth, openness, the ability to deal with
conflict, loneliness, and the imperfection of all human effort. And that is faith. Without faith both courage and love
become impossible. I use the word "faith" in its most
primordial sense. It is the conviction that despite distraction, discouragement, disappointment, failure, disillusion-
ment, and frustration, it is still worth the effort to try to
love and to be loved. Faith in this sense is a fully conscious
commitment to the idea that life has worth and purpose
and value. If one does not believe in the value of human
life and the dignity of human effort, then one will simply
not have the courage it takes to keep alive wonder and
surprise, to engage in conflict and its resolution, to give
and receive affection in a love relationship. The faith I
have described is prereligious in the sense that we experience it at the core of our being before we use religious
symbols to give expression to such a fundamental assurance of our own value and worth. Our religious symbols
and myths, as Schubert Ogden has pointed out, are merely
ways of re-presenting and reassuring us of this basic worth
that is at the very core of the structure of our existence
and awareness. Some religious symbols are more effective
than others at re-presenting this primal assurance, and,
of course, no religious symbol is so effective that we cannot turn away from that basic assurance and lead lives of
grim, monotonous despair. All too many people assert religious symbols but live lives that give every evidence that
the symbol is not taken too seriously as a way of viewing
the world.

Schubert Ogden (*The Reality of God and Other Essays,*

New York, Harper & Row, 1966, p. 116) has argued that there are two fundamental presuppositions to religious commitment:

> First, that life as we live it is somehow of ultimate worth; and, second, that it is possible to understand our selves and the world in their relation to totality so that this assurance of life's worth may be reasonably affirmed. Therefore, the criterion for assessing the truth of myths may be formulated as follows: *mythical assertions are true insofar as they so explicate our unforfeitable assurance that life is worthwhile that the understanding of faith they represent cannot be falsified by the essential conditions of life itself.*

The question, then, we must ask about our religious symbols is that when we "put them on" and view the world from their perspective, does this perspective reinforce our own fundamental self-assurance? And does it also enable us to interpret and to cope with the ambiguities of our existence? Those of us who are Christians must ask ourselves what the core of those symbols sheds on the ambiguities, the strains, the conflicts, the tensions, the demands of human love.

The central symbol of Christianity is the combination of the cross and resurrection. Jesus who died now lives. How can that symbol possibly shed any light on the complexities and ambiguities of human sexual relationships?

I am afraid that one must say that it ought to be obvious how the cross and resurrection are pertinent to human sexuality. That it is not obvious comments not on the ineffectiveness of the symbol but on our own prudery and fear. The Christians of early Rome, who transferred the pagan spring fertility rite of plunging the candle into water, had no such difficulties. They knew that the lighted candle represented the penis and that water represented a vagina and a womb; and they knew, too, that their pagan friends and neighbors performed this rite in order to guarantee the fertility of their fields, their animals, and their wives. The early Christians thought that when Christ rose from the dead, he consumated his union with his bride, the church. If the resurrection looked like a sexual symbol then and does not look like one to us, the reason, perhaps, is that they had a much clearer realization than we do that life presumes fertility.

The cross and resurrection in their very core mean to us that life triumphs over death, but that we must die first. New life comes from being reborn, not from escaping the necessity and the pain of death. When we put on this cross-resurrection symbol we are then able to see that each new conflict, each new risk, each new thrust against loneliness is a death that we must endure if we have hope to live anew. The young lover must give death to his fears if he is to shout at his wife that she should open her eyes and look at him. But unless he is willing to die that death, he will never experience the resurrection that a sexually responsive wife would make possible. Similarly, the young wife who must take her husband's hand and firmly guide it must die a thousand deaths to her shame and prudery. But there is no escaping from this death if she wishes to have a new life of sexual arousal and satisfaction.

The middle-aged couple who tentatively and awkwardly begin to exchange tenderness and affection as a prelude to beginning their love affair all over again, or perhaps starting it for the first time, must go through the anguish of the damned (or something like it) to put aside the hurts and the resentments and the bitterness of the past. Only by dying to the mistakes and anger of the past can they expect to rise to a new life of affection and pleasure.

Everyone must die to the prudery and shame that makes them shy and awkward if they are going to rise to a new life in which erotic self-display surrounds them with an ambiance of wonder and surprise. The woman approaching her husband with her nakedness covered only by a martini pitcher must die to the humiliating possibility that her husband won't be interested and will attempt to brush her off. The new dimension of sexual pleasure that her surprise can make possible will only in fact be a form of resurrection if she is determined to cope with a brush-off by telling him that either he instantaneously remove his clothes and make love to her or she will pour the martinis over his head and call a divorce lawyer.

A healthy genital relationship is one in which the two partners are engaged in the ongoing process of attracting and luring one another to bed. The conquest is never so complete, the surrender never so definitive that it need not be repeated. When the lover ceases to be a challenge, when he yields his body for pleasure with no effort on the partner's part, the game becomes uninteresting. Similarly, when a lover is permitted to take pleasure without having to lure, then the response is perfunctory, given almost as though something else were on the partner's mind. Genitality without mutual luring loses most of its eroticism; it becomes passionless passion.

When a man never sees a look of anticipation and invitation in his woman's eyes, and when she never feels his hand squeeze her thigh as she sits next to him in the car or pat her bottom as she climbs the steps ahead of him, their relationship has become dull and routine. Yet the necessity of winning one's partner over and over again is wearying. A comfortable, unexciting routine requires less effort, and it provides much less payoff.

The surprise component of sex has as its principal purpose the arousal of the other so that in his excitement he will pursue us. So, too, with Yahweh's intervention in human events. He surprises us in order that he might attract us. He excites us so that we might be drawn out of our mundane lives and pursue him. The Hound of Heaven image works both ways: God pursues us by attracting us to pursue him. But then that is the way every passionate lover acts.

Our Greek philosophy pictures God for us as the "unmoved mover." Our dull, dry catechetics has described him as a dispassionate judge who is sufficient unto himself and does not need us. But contemporary process theology, reflecting the scriptures, describes him as a "tender companion" (to use Alfred North Whitehead's term) who attracts us to follow along with him by his gentle and seductive lures.

When a man and a woman practice their mutual wiles on one another they are imitating the way God works on us; and to the extent that these wiles draw them both out of their mundane narrowness, they are literally cooperating with God's gentle seductions. The more the lover excites the partner into a frenzy of passion, the more godlike he is. This is not merely exaggerated rhetoric; if we take the scriptural imagery seriously—and we must—it is literal truth.

A wife who passively accepts her husband's advances and never takes the initiative and who is "uninterested" in sex may think she is a dutiful woman and even something of a martyr. In fact she is not only dull and somewhat frigid, she has repressed the spark of divinity that abides in her female body. And the husband who "leaves his wife alone" except when the demand for tension release is irresistible may think he is a kind and considerate mate; but unless he can make his wife's body writhe in joy and her voice shout with uncontrolled pleasure, he is a failure as a man and is false to the power of the divinity that lurks in his body.

It is a mistake to think that God's love for us is the mild, circumspect *agape,* a bloodless, "nice" affection from which all passion has been drained. The God of the Testaments, New and Old, is not a "nice" God at all but a lover consumed with *eros.* It is disgraceful for his followers to mate with each other in any but the most fervent, erotic way. The greater the pleasure that man and woman give to each other—in bed and in every dimension of their relationship—the more is God present with them.

Does the cross-resurrection symbolism really apply to these events? Or is it merely an almost blasphemous distortion of the Jesus myth to say that the cross and resurrection give meaning and purpose to the anguish and ecstasy of human sexual encounter? One is forced to reply that if the cross-resurrection symbolism does not apply to such poignant and frequent human situations, it is not much good. But of course it does apply, for it tells us in the most dramatic religious terms possible that human growth comes through death and rebirth, and that it is safe to take the risk of dying because God has guaranteed us rebirth. If man need not fear the death that comes at the end of life, he surely need not fear the death of fear, uncertainty, and anxiety, which are a part of every important interpersonal encounter in his life.

I am not suggesting that the cross-resurrection symbol is the only religious symbol that says life is worth living. Neither would I wish to argue that it is necessarily the most powerful (though my own personal convictions would affirm its supreme power). I am merely suggesting that such arguments are foolish. The cross-resurrection symbol, which is at the core of the religious belief of every Christian, is readily available to Christians as an antidote to the fear and the suspicion that stand in the way of love.

Or to put the matter more graphically: when two naked lovers stand in each other's presence in that basic, fear-filled and delight-filled human encounter, they are, if they are Christians, symbolically clad in the cross and the resurrection of Jesus. And if they are willing to look at each other and at themselves through the powerful light that that symbol sheds, they become far more attractive than they would be without it, because the symbol tells them that it is all right to take risks. Their Christian commitment assures them that they need not be afraid of the deaths they are going to have to die if their love is to continue and to grow. Those deaths are but a prelude to new life.

"Putting on" the symbols of the cross and resurrection of Jesus ought to make a man and woman far more sexy than putting on mint green underwear (though there's nothing wrong with that either). If the cross and resurrection do not make us more sexually attractive, that is not Jesus' fault. It's ours.